Travellers' Tales

ROAD TO THE ISLES

HISTORY   LEGENDS   LANDMARKS
LORE AND STRANGE SECRETS

LANG SYNE
PUBLISHING

25 10 = miles

KYLE of
LOCHALSH

SKYE

EILEAN DONNAN
Dornie
LOCH
DUICH

Kintail
Shiel Bdge.
Glenelg
GLEN
SHIEL

GLEN
AFFRIC

Cluanie
Inn

A 87

LOCH
CLUANIE

A 8

LOCH
HOURN

LOCH
QUOICH

Tomdoun

LOCH
LOCH

Mallaig

LOCH
ARKAIG

A 830   Corpach

INVE

LOCH
EIL

Fort
William

A 828

to
Ballachulish

INVERNESS

A82

DOCHFOUR HOUSE

862

Drumnadrochit

CASTLE URQUHART

LOCH MEIKLE

Dores

Roderick
Mackenzie
Memorial

LOCH NESS

Invermoriston

Inverfarigaig

Foyers

GLEN MORISTON

Dundreggan

CALEDONIAN CANAL

Fort Augustus

EN RRY

LOCH OICH

WELL of the SEVEN HEADS

A82

Spean Bridge

CHY

(after the Massacre of Glencoe)

N NEVIS

ncoe

N

W

E

S

PUBLISHER'S NOTE

This material is reprinted from "The Highlands and their Legends" by Otta F. Swire first published by Oliver and Boyd in 1963. Lang Syne Publishers Ltd. would like to thank the author's son, Dr Jim Swire, and his sister Mrs Flora Gardner, for granting permission to publish this edition.

Otta Swire spent much of her childhood in the Highlands, chiefly in Easter Ross, Slye and Kingussie. She also spent a lot of time in Glen Urquahart and in her girlhood the family lived near Inverness

Published by Lang Syne Publishers Ltd., Clydebank G81 1QF in 1992 and printed by Darnley Press Ltd., Clydebank G81 1QF.

FACTUAL UPDATES

When the book was first written the Great Glen Cattle Ranch and the hydro-electric scheme were new features of the Highland scene. The author's prediction that the Ranch "may do much for the Highlands" (page 40) came to pass. It did much to fuel the local economy and was later split into several independent units.

In the Forest of Cluanie (page 60) the deer did indeed survive the changes brought by the new form of power; the herds continue to thrive but have been driven more into the hills lately by new road developments.

Other changes: Ness Castle (page 30) is now self catering holiday accommodation, the Dores Inn (page 31) is under different ownership, a fine bridge displaced the ferry (page 45), and the school at Balmacarra (page 77) is now used by the Navy.

Dedication by
Dr. Jim Swire

I am glad to see these legends reprinted in 1991 for the traveller on the 'Road to the Isles'. For my mother, Otta Swire the destination was always Skye which her scholarly father, Sir William Tarn, also loved so much, and where she and Roger Swire played in childhood, later marrying in Inverness.

Roger Swire's mother was a McDonald and directly descended from the Flora McDonald who rescued Bonnie Prince Charlie from the English redcoats, rowing with him to Skye as in the famous Scottish

Flora MacDonald Swire

song. Otta's only daughter, my sister, was christened Flora McDonald Swire. My elder daughter was also christened Flora McDonald Swire, and loved Skye dearly, spending much of her childhood holidays at Orbost House, near Dunvegan; for many years the family home.

This last Flora's young life, so loving, so vivacious and so full of talent, was snuffed out on the day before her twenty-fourth birthday over the little border town of Lockerbie, on the 21st December 1988, by the hand of some alien impersonal asassin, who knew neither of her nor her proud and gentle heritage. Her ashes are buried beside the grave of her grandmother in the little cemetary at Caroy on the Sligachan to Dunvegan road. She lives in the minds of her sister, her brother and her parents; in the words of her stone "longed for always".

Soak up the peace of Skye, for there is never peace among men. As her grandmother, Otta, would have wished, we dedicate this book to our Flora.

7

INTRODUCTION

Who flooded the valley to create Loch Ness? What are the secrets of Eilean Donan Castle? Where is the Bay of the Dead Men? How did a church bell ring itself to trap a murderer? Why was the severed head of one of Bonnie Prince Charlie's friends sent to England in a brine tub? When did Loch Oich get a monster and Loch Lochy a water goddess?

These are just some of the fascinating questions answered by Otta F. Swire in the course of this magical journey from Inverness and Ballachulish to Kyle of Localsh, gateway to the misty and beautiful Isle of Skye.

En route we meet the Black Devil, the Speckled Devil and the White Devil of Glen Urquhart, the ghosts at war in Glen Shiel, the Glenmoriston fairies who stole babies, the Robin Hood of Loch Ness and the giant yellow horse on its shores that carried off little boys.

We learn how to outwit a witch, hear about the herd of cattle that just kept growing and growing no matter how many cows its owner gave away, discover why Castle Urquhart had the reputation of being a pirates' stronghold and why 10 foot tall giants used to roam Glenelg.

There is the grim story behind the castle of ghosts, the story of a frigate launched on Loch Ness to tame lawless locals, theories on origins of names like Loch Ness and Fort Augustus, the murderer who used Highland hospitality to avoid paying the penalty of his crime, the Fort Augustus monks who grew too lazy to cultivate the land, the fights, murders and cattle raids in the Great Glen that lasted from Roman times until the '45, plus many more fascinating stories from the country that has some of the best and most beautiful scenery in Britain.

LOCH NESS

From reining of the Water horse
That bounded till the waves were foaming,
Watching the infant tempest's course,
Chasing the sea-snake in his roaming

    ★   ★   ★   ★   ★

Children of wild Thule, we.

SIR WALTER SCOTT

'NESS' is believed to be an early Pictish word, its meaning unknown. It probably first belonged to the River Ness and may have been the name of some ancient goddess. There are, however, many tales purporting to explain or account for it.

In the very early days, it is said, there was no loch in the Great Glen; instead, the land now under water held many farms and homesteads, for the Glen was then a dry and fertile valley, a giver of plenty to its inhabitants. In the middle of the valley was a spring of magic virtue guarded by a strict taboo. Whoever came to draw water from this well must remove the stone, draw water and *immediately* replace the stone, no matter how long a queue of would-be water drawers might be waiting, 'or else—!' One day a woman went alone to the well for water and as she removed the stone she heard her child scream as if in agony or great fear. She dropped the stone and ran. After her ran the water, for the well instantly overflowed and shortly filled the long valley. The people of the valley fled to the hills, crying as they ran: 'Tha loch nis ann, tha loch nis ann' (There is a loch there now). Hence its name.

The western side of Inverness is in the old 'parish' of Bona. This is said to have taken its name from the ferry across the River Ness near Dochfour, soon after the river leaves the loch. The ferry was called Ban-àth or white ford and Dr Watson believes it was named from the white stones in the water there. There is still a small white beach close by. Local tradition makes it one of these white stones that St. Columba is related in Adamnan's *Life of St. Columba* to have sent to King Brude. In the *Life* it is told how Broichan, the Druid and the foster-father of King Brude, held a maidservant captive and how St. Columba had pity on the girl and ordered him to free her, but Broichan refused. Then the saint said: 'Know, Broichan, know that if you refuse to deliver to me this captive stranger before I leave this Province you will surely die.' And this he said in the presence of Brude the King. Then St. Columba departed and began his journey home to Iona. When he came to the River Ness he lifted from the water a white pebble and, holding it up in the clear sunlight, he told all who were with him to look well at it for it was a stone which should cure many. Then he told them that Broichan was 'smitten by an angel and severely ill and would soon free the maid'. Two horsemen, riding hard, soon overtook St. Columba's party, bringing the news which the saint had foretold. Broichan, they said, was willing to free the girl and Brude had sent them to beg that the saint would return to the aid of the King's foster-father who was very ill. But St. Columba would not, saying the time had now come when he must leave that place. However, he sent two of his monks to the king, with the stone and with the word: 'If Broichan is willing first to free the girl, let this stone be dipped in water and give him to drink and he will recover. But if he opposes the freeing of the slave-girl he will die immediately.'

The two monks, very frightened, went to the king. The Druid immediately freed the girl, drank water in which the stone was dipped, and recovered. The stone floated on the water 'contrary to its nature'. The stone was preserved by the king and cured many, but when a man's time came to die the stone could never be found although it was kept, carefully guarded, among the king's treasures. Thus it was sought in vain on the day of the death of King Brude in 583.

St. Columba visited Brude on more than one occasion but, not unnaturally after this matter of the slave girl, both he and his visits were far from popular with the king's foster-father. Broichan felt that the saint had made him lose face and he planned to regain his old ascendancy. He asked St. Columba on one occasion when he proposed to journey home. 'On the third day, God willing and life remaining, we propose to begin our voyage,' answered the saint. 'You will not be able to do so,' replied the Druid, 'for I can make the wind contrary for you and bring clouds upon you.' The saint replied that God rules all things and they will do as He directs. On the third day St. Columba and his monks, with a large crowd following them, set out for Loch Ness but when they reached the water's edge 'a great darkness descended upon the water with contrary winds and tempest'. St. Columba called upon God and entered the boat which awaited him and as the sailors hesitated in fear, knowing well the Loch's treacheries, he bade them make sail. Then the watching crowd saw the boat borne rapidly in the right direction against the contrary winds and then the winds themselves veering round to the direction desired by the saint. So he and his monks reached the further end of the Loch swiftly and without mishap.

To traverse the Great Glen is to make in a sense a pilgrimage for it was by this chain of lochs—Loch Linnhe, Loch Lochy, Loch Oich, Loch Ness—that St. Columba and his monks came to visit King Brude, or, as one might say, by this chain of lochs Christianity came to the Highlands. It is told how they once stopped to rest and eat not far from what is now Foyers. As they rested they saw a party of evil men approaching and St. Columba, knowing that they were searching for him to kill him, bade his monks raise their voices in a hymn he had composed, known since as the Hymn of the Deer. They obeyed and God deafened the ears of his enemies so that the hymn appeared to them as herds of deer calling. 'Where deer call, men are not,' said the leader and he and his men paddled away from that shore. Legend says, however, that St. Columba had supernatural aid of another sort also on his first journey. Here is the story.

Since there were then no roads St. Columba and his monks had to journey over heather-clad hills and through a part of the Caledonian Forest as best they could, carrying their coracles. Thankful indeed were they when they reached each loch in turn and were able to sail down it. But the weather was stormy and by the time they arrived at Loch Ness, that 30-mile long sheet of

11

water covered with white-capped waves looked anything but inviting to the tired men. Suddenly among the tossing white wave crests appeared a black head—it was the Waterhorse of Loch Ness come to pay his duty to St. Columba, and a handsome great stallion he was though not unduly wise. He swam up to the saint to offer his service, but it was some time before he understood what the monks' boats were for or that they were attempting to row themselves down the length of the great loch against the wind. Once he had grasped the situation, however, he took charge in a most practical manner. Explaining that he needed hands, he assumed the form of an athletic young man, seized the painters of each coracle and strung them together on to one large withy, then, resuming horse form, he took the withy between his strong teeth and swam rapidly off. Almost before they knew it the saint and his party were landing in comfort on the little white sheltered beach at the eastern end of the loch. Here St. Columba blessed the Each Uisge and gave him the freedom of Loch Ness for ever.

But it was not only the help and blessing of a Saint that this waterhorse coveted; he is also reputed to have made a pact with the Devil. But the Devil got the better of him. The waterhorse was very much worried by the belief that as the River Ness ran through Loch Ness and as no waterhorse can cross over running water he could never pass from one side of his own loch to the other. The Devil promised him that if he would give him one ride every year over any water he (the Devil) might choose to name, he in return would ensure that every drop of water the river brought into the loch it would carry out again, and not a drop more. To do this the river water must flow strictly in its own path on the loch surface and the Each Uisge could dive under it in safety. What the Devil did not tell, and the waterhorse did not know, was that this was in any case the law enforced on all Highland rivers from olden times when what might perhaps be described as The Amalgamated Union of Waterhorses and Waterbulls had made just such a pact with the Evil One to cover all rivers that passed through a loch, that running waters might not trouble the loch creatures. And it had been made with no promise of service to the Devil in return. It is certainly curious that these waterhorses, lords not only of many a loch but also of many a river pool, should not dare to cross a river, and even more curious that the Devil should be supposed to have power over all rivers. But running water has strange powers. It is not only waterhorses which dare not cross it. No witch may cross running water either, neither may the fairies (anyhow, not when pursuing mortals), nor a ghost, though ghosts may go as far across a river that is bridged as the keystone of the bridge but no further. The sea, however, is evidently quite crossable by ghosts, for 'Big Donald of the Ghosts' fled from his besetting spectre to America and found his ghost already there awaiting his arrival. 'How did you come here?' he cried in amaze. 'Oh, I came round about; the ghost's trick,' replied the imperturbable spectre.

Everyone knows that 'He will have no luck who takes a cat across a stream.'

From time immemorial Loch Ness has been a 'queer' loch with 'queer' stories of its inhabitants. There are stories of a Something, very old and evil, which once lived in its depths and to whom sacrifices were made—sacrifices generally of cattle, sometimes in the dim past of children, flung in withy baskets into its waters. I used to hear in my childhood, when we often visited Glen Urquhart, that this 'thing' was still sometimes seen, a great dark shapeless mass, brooding over the waters, dreaming of evil. And its dreams worked, for if it was seen, however faint and formless an apparition, shortly afterwards someone would be drowned and their body would never be found. There were several schools of thought about this last fact, for fact it apparently is that a body lost in Loch Ness is never, or very rarely, seen again. In olden times, 'it' claimed them; later came the idea that Loch Ness had a central hole which went deeper than anything else in Scotland, perhaps in the world, and into this bottomless pit all lost things were drawn. Dr Johnson records that on his visit he was told that the loch was 140 fathoms deep. Some said the 'deep' had an outlet to the sea, others that it connected with an equally deep hole in Lough Long in Ireland. The great cavern, said others, contained a Monster, or many Monsters, slimy white eyeless creatures that never saw the light. When Loch Ness was being sounded for the building of the Caledonian Canal the ship's sounding line ran right out somewhere between Invermoriston and Drumnadrochit and did not reach bottom. This at once revived the belief in the bottomless abyss there. In vain the engineers concerned explained that the line they were using was of no great length, they having only wished to ascertain that ships of a draught suitable for the Canal could be sure of enough water in Loch Ness; how much more depth there was did not concern them. However, as considerable interest was aroused a longer sea-sounding line was borrowed and let down. It too failed to reach bottom it was said, and so the old belief in the bottomless pit was reinforced with a story that it had proved deeper than anything known in the ocean. I am told it has now been exactly charted and is 'deep for a loch'.

Tales of the great eyeless monsters also persist. We have 'Nessie' of course, who has been seen and described by too many reliable witnesses whose testimony cannot be ignored for her existence to be doubted but who, alas!, has also been seen and described by so many unreliable witnesses that she has become an impossible joke to the general public. One of the nicest of the stories of this kind came from an excited family from a Lancashire town who in the days before the Second World War claimed to have seen 'Nessie' leave the water and conceal herself in the bracken 'to await her prey'. She was a terrible creature covered with red hair, with fearsome horns and chewing something from which blood dripped as she chewed. A brave policeman returned with them to beard her in her lair and found it not such a bad description, if you leave out the dripping blood, of a rather nice red Highland cow chewing the cud in a bracken bed.

A more horrible origin for the 'eyeless ones' seems to be great eels. That these live and grow to an exceptionally large size in Loch Ness is not disputed. Many years ago, before 'Nessie' had been heard of, a visitor was drowned in the Loch and her husband, determined to recover her body, hired a diver. After one descent the diver refused to return to the water, saying that the eels made the risk too great. The husband said he was 'a local man and just superstitious' and appealed to the Navy at Invergordon. A naval diving party was sent and the first man down signalled to come up almost at once and said the eels were too dangerous; he could not protect his air line. The husband repeated 'superstition' and, being both rich and obstinate, got a diving party up from the London docks and met them at the station to avoid their hearing 'eel gossip'. They also refused to remain in the water because of 'the great eels trying to foul their air lines and wrap themselves round them'. They were reputed to have said that they never before saw such creatures and that to remain in their company was suicide and to send divers down among them was murder. What there really is or is not in the depths beneath the waters of Scotland's largest loch is still a question, but from time immemorial 'it', whatever 'it' is, has had an evil and terrifying reputation very different from that enjoyed by the ordinary waterhorse. No doubt the facts that storms rise to a dangerous pitch with little warning on such a long, narrow piece of water and that the Great Glen has always been a weak point for earth tremors may have added to its reputation both for evil and for beauty. On a still day it is *very* beautiful, especially in spring and autumn, and on a wild day magnificent.

The Feinn also have a connection with the Glen.* Once Fionn put himself under promise to the Big Lad that if the Big Lad would serve him for a year and a day Fionn would accompany him to a feast to be held in the palace of the King of Lochlann and that 'he would not take with him a dog or a man, a calf or a child, a weapon or an adversary, but would go himself alone'. When the day came for them to go Fionn was heavy of heart for he saw well that it was a trap. He bade the Feinn seek him in Lochlann in a year and a day and told them 'to hold one great day on the strand of Lochlann' to avenge him if he had not returned. These things they promised. But as he made ready to start his fool spoke to him and asked if he would take the advice of a fool. 'What is that?' enquired Fionn courteously. 'Take Bran's gold chain with you,' said the fool, 'for it is not a dog or a man, a calf or a child, a weapon or an adversary.' Fionn, saying fools are often wise, agreed. At great speed he and the Big Lad travelled to the palace of the King of Lochlann and by the time they arrived Fionn was weary. The King and his lords were all seated, discussing how best to put Fionn to death. 'What,' asked the King, 'is the most shameful death a Fiann can die?' 'Let us

* The story of the Feinn is told on page 80.

15

hang him,' cried some. 'No, burn him,' said others. 'Drown him,' advised another. Then one rose and said: 'The most disgraceful death a Fiann can die is to be killed by a cur of a dog. Let us send him unarmed into Glen More where the Grey Dog will kill him.' And all cried: 'To face the Grey Dog, that is the death for Fionn.'

Now Grey Dog was blood-brother to Fionn's dog Bran and he belonged to the Brave Young Hero. But a chief of the men of Lochlann had once found the Brave Young Hero alone by the sea-shore and he and his crew had captured him and claimed the dog as his ransom. The chief took the dog to the King of Lochlann but the animal went mad for grief at the loss of his master. So he was sent back to Scotland and was turned loose to run wild in the Great Glen.

The men of Lochlann took Fionn to the mouth of the Glen and there, when they could hear the howling of Grey Dog, they left him. Grey Dog came down the glen howling and foaming, with his tongue out to one side of his mouth and his eyes glaring, like the mad thing he was. So hot was his breath that each snort of his nostrils burned everything, trees, heather, creatures, for three miles on either side of him and for three miles before him. He looked at Fionn and snorted. The heat tormented Fionn. It was unbearable. He plunged into Loch Ness and hid in its waters. Then, as Grey Dog drew near, he raised one arm out of the water and shook Bran's gold chain towards Grey Dog. Grey Dog saw the chain and knew it. He wagged his tail and came to Fionn. Fionn left the water and caressed Grey Dog, and Grey Dog licked Fionn's burns that he had made with his breath 'from top of head to sole of foot'. Then Fionn put Bran's gold chain round his neck and together they walked down the Glen. Near the Glen's mouth was a little house where dwelt an old man and an old woman who used to feed Grey Dog. They saw Fionn coming with Grey Dog and the old man said: 'Though the people of Lochlann and of Ireland were assembled, among them all there would not be a man who could do that but Fionn, King of the Feinn and Bran's chain of gold with him.' They offered Fionn hospitality. Fionn told the old man his tale and he told the old woman and it pleased her, so that she said Fionn might rest in her house till the end of the year and a day, and Grey Dog with him. This they did. On the last day of the year and a day an 'innumerable host' appeared on the strand. It was the Feinn come to search for or to avenge their King. Fionn and Grey Dog strode to meet them. Very great joy was theirs in the host when they met Fionn and very great joy of meeting between Bran and Grey Dog. They took vengeance on the men of Lochlann. Indeed 'They began at one end of Lochlann and stopped not till they came out at the other.' Then they went home to the hall of Fionn and 'held a merry feast for a day and a year'.

Castle Urquhart

INVERNESS
TO FORT AUGUSTUS

From the ruined castle wall
That nods to the darkened moon,
'Tis an old time song comes faintly along
Like the sough of a fairy's croon.
MURDOCH MACLEAN

THE GREAT GLEN has had the honour to be classified in the U.S.A. guides as one of the four things which every visitor to Britain must see, and it is certainly worthy of note. It is definitely more satisfying to travel through it by water if possible because the two roads which run one on either side of the Loch show only the opposite shore. The hills are too close and too steep to be seen from directly below.

The Glen has always had a rather sinister reputation and this is hardly to be wondered at perhaps in view of its history, for it has seen much fighting and for many centuries. Indeed, if tradition is to be believed, from Roman times until the '45 there can scarcely have been a single month in which it did not see a fight, a murder or a cattle-raid. A line of ancient forts protected it, some vitrified, others of the 'dun' type. These still await scientific excavation, so their exact age is not known, but all are believed to date back at least to the bronze age and some may be older.

The first road down the north shore of Loch Ness from Inverness to Drumnadrochit was made by Sir James Grant when wheeled vehicles appeared in the North in the middle of the eighteenth century. He was known as 'the good Sir James'. The present road was engineered in the early nineteenth century by Telford, the builder of the Caledonian Canal, whose name and work are commemorated in Telford Street and Telford Road in Inverness. This road was an enormous boon to the county but

19

it was very narrow, and twisty beyond belief. There was a stretch of ten miles between Drumnadrochit and Invermoriston on which two cars could not pass, and fifteen miles of it had to have a speed limit of 12 miles per hour. So the present wider road was blasted out of the rock face, a big undertaking most fortunately finished just before the last war. Before 'good Sir James' there was nothing but the old grass road across the hills by Abriachan which may well go back to the stone age but is simply a drove road.

The present road crosses the Canal to the west of Inverness, passing close to Tom-na-hurich and then on beneath the shadow of Torbhean—one of the old vitrified forts and a wonderful sight when the trees have their autumn colouring; indeed the whole road should be seen then. It passes Craig Dunain, the tragically large mental hospital which yet is not large enough, and then Dunain itself where once an old dun could be seen and where an evil hag keeps watch, hoping for chances to destroy any of the name of MacDougall, and on to the end of the River Ness where the Castle of Bona once guarded the pass.

The rich lands and, especially, herds of the Glen were a great temptation to the clans of the West with their poor pasture land, so cattle-lifting raids were common. When Hector Buie Maclean became Warden of Bona and Urquhart Castles for Alexander, Lord of the Isles, he determined to put an end to the raids by raiding Lochaber in return. This he did while Lochiel was absent in Ireland with his men. Maclean killed and plundered without mercy, then retreated along the south shore of the Loch to Castle Bona with his plunder and his captives. Lochiel, on his return from Ireland, at once pursued him with a large force of the western clans. Hector threatened to kill his prisoners if Lochiel did not retreat; Lochiel, who had by this time captured Hector's two sons and several of his followers, offered to exchange prisoners. Maclean refused and at once carried out his threat to kill all the prisoners in his hands. The furious Camerons replied by hanging his two sons and the other Urquhart men in front of the Castle. In the ensuing battle Hector Maclean was killed. The ghosts of both sets of prisoners were supposed to haunt the Castle, joined together in hatred of their human murderers, and it became known no longer as Castle Bona but as Caisteal Spioradan, Castle of the Ghosts or Spirits. Soon, no one could be found willing to garrison it and it fell into ruins. The ghosts then took to venting their spite on any passing traveller, however innocent of murder he might be, and there was general relief in the neighbourhood when the ruins were demolished to make way for the Caledonian Canal.

In Commonwealth days it was from Bona that the first frigate to sail Loch Ness set out. Cromwell, when he built his Citadel in Inverness, intended it to be the centre of a peaceful and well-ordered countryside and proceeded, as was his wont, to make it so. The memory of the law and order which he enforced still lingers in pleasant contrast to the murder and rape of Cumberland's 'Hanoverian occupation'. Cromwell found all the clans in arms, many making use of the disorders of the day to plunder their neighbours. His troops found the country difficult and complained that marauders constantly escaped across the loch in small boats they had hidden in the reeds or even on blown-up sheep skins. So the order was given: 'Put a frigate on the lake.' Just like that! The ship was brought to Inverness under sail, there she was dismantled as far as possible and a sort of wooden cage was built round her to hold her upright; this was then set on rollers made of pines felled for the purpose and three companies of troops manhandled her, on these clumsy rollers, from Inverness to Bona (there was no road then, remember!) where she was refitted and put to 'sea'. Few things can ever have created such excitement in the Glen or indeed throughout the North, and a lovely sight she must have been flying down the Loch, her white sails against the green of the woods and blue of the hills. It is recorded of her that she carried 60 men in all, and stores, from one end of the loch to the other 'in a few hours'.

To return to the road. This next passes Dochfour with its small lakes and lovely gardens. This part is well worth a visit in spring, just to see the masses of daffodils, and later of flowering shrubs, running down to the water. After Dochfour great Loch Ness herself bursts upon the view and from there on the scenery is indescribably beautiful at almost any season and in most weather. This stretch of road and hillside used to be a great haunt of snakes, not only the harmless grass snake but also the poisonous viper. On any warm day one could count on seeing at least half a dozen sunning themselves on the rocks beside the road. Then Baroness Burton decided to keep goats and a flock of beautiful silky white ones appeared. The fashion spread and soon goats of all sizes and colours wandered about the hillside and now there appear to be no snakes, or, to be fair, few goats either. It has long been held by serious farmers that goats do rid a countryside of snakes, and legend has it that goats like eating snakes. They are said, when they find one, to put a hoof on its head and then begin to eat it

"... used to be a great haunt of snakes ..."

from the tail up, uttering plaintive, unhappy little cries all the time as though they found the wriggling of the snake unpleasant. They may well do so. Goats are queer creatures. So of course are snakes. It is most unlucky not to kill every snake you meet. If you don't, it may later kill or bewitch you. But, no matter what you do, no snake will die till the sun sets. Goats' milk was highly prized in the Highlands: we hear,

> Garlic with May butter
> Cureth all disease
> But drink of goats' white milk
> At the same time as these,

and also,

Wash thy face with a lotion of goats' milk and sweet violets and there's not a King's son but will then run after thee.

The road passes Temple Pier where the little loch steamer called regularly on its way to and from Inverness and Fort William. Above the pier there is a crag and a hollow, both believed to have been sacred spots in the old pagan days. In the hollow was a healing spring, once the abode of a god or goddess. When St. Columba brought Christianity to the Highlands he is reputed to have dealt gently (and wisely) with old pagan gods and demons who were worshipped in groves and springs and lakes throughout the glens. He explained to his converts that these spirits were under One God, just creatures as we are. If a spring could heal the sick, let us thank God for this blessing He has sent us and build a church or cell near by in which to give continued thanks. If an evil spirit troubled certain waters, the saint would bless them and drive away the evil in God's name and, once again, build a church to protect men. So here the pagan sacred spot was blessed and a tiny church was built in honour of St. Finan. This St. Finan was a contemporary and companion of Columba and became the chief saint of this district. Later again, a bigger church was built on the site, this time in honour of St. Ninian. The healing well held pride of place beside each in turn and each seems to have been known as Teampuill St. So-and-so, but which gave its name to Temple Pier is not clear.

The story is told that St. Finan, as an old man, desired to ride from Temple Hollow to his church on Loch Lochy. He set out alone and most unfortunately his horse caught its foot in a rabbit hole and came down, breaking its leg. The old saint was helpless. He was too far from either church to reach them on foot and no one knew his whereabouts. He knelt down to pray and await death but his prayers were disturbed by a soft nose nuzzling his ear. He looked and, behold, a red deer stag stood by him. Breviary in hand, he mounted his new steed and was soon delivered safely at his church on Loch Lochy side.

Not far from Temple Pier the Glen Urquhart road takes off to the right in the middle of Drumnadrochit while the main road turns round a small bay and passes over the headland on which the ruins of Castle Urquhart are to be seen, down by the water's edge. Once a great stronghold with a fleet of galleys which controlled the Loch, the Castle has now fallen upon evil days. Where once its owners grew rich on tolls from every boat which passed up or down this, the main waterway of a roadless Highlands, tourists now pay a small entrance fee to the Board of Ancient Monuments.* But perhaps it is poetic justice, for the Castle galleys

* Now Historic Scotland.

were supposed, in return for prompt payment of tolls, to ensure safe passage for all boats traversing the loch, and fear of robbers, outlaws and pirates made boat owners willing to pay for protection, but it was said that under these conditions piracy ceased to be worth while and that then the Castle galleys had to do a bit of it themselves on the side to keep the tolls going. Others said bitterly that the Castle was nothing better than a pirate stronghold and never had been. It was subsidised competition that drove the 'free' pirates off the water!

Actually the Castle has a history of wars and sieges second to none in Scotland. It was an important stronghold because it controlled the Great Glen, a main route between East and West, and between the years 1160 and 1398 it changed hands at least sixteen times, although several of the different holders claimed to 'hold it for the King'. It ceased to be a royal fortress in 1509 when the King made a gift of it to the Grant of the day, known as the Red Bard. According to tradition the Castle was built by an Irishman, Conachar (or O'Chonachar) MacNessa, a prince of Ulster, in the twelfth century. Conachar himself is a half-legendary figure reputed, on the one hand, to have received the land and the dun which preceded the Castle on that headland from King Malcolm IV as a reward for his help in the war of 1160 against the Highlanders and to have immediately enlarged the dun into a Castle and greatly strengthened it, and on the other hand to be the son of an Irish goddess Nessa who, according to this story, gave her name to Loch Ness. In this version Conachar called upon the witches of the Glen to help him build his castle and the witches hewed and carried every block of stone used for the walls. They brought it in part from Abriachan and in part from Caiplich but they were very angry indeed at the task. How Conachar forced them into it is not known, but the spot from which they first sighted the castle on each heavily-laden journey was known as Cragan nam Mallachd, the Rock of the Curses, within living memory. The witches of the Glen were both numerous and powerful—it was a famous witch centre—and they used to meet and hold their 'Sabbaths' on An Clairach, the Harp, a rock on the shore of Loch Ness near the farm of Tychat. Here Satan used to sit and play for them every 12th of May (old May Day) that they might dance for his pleasure; hence the rock's name. The witches' curses on Castle Urquhart seem to have been fulfilled, judging from its subsequent history.

Conachar of Castle Urquhart possessed a great dog which grew old and stiff and he decided to kill it but was prevented by a woman who approached him as he went out to hunt and said: 'Let the dog live: his own day awaits him', and disappeared. Realising that it is never wise to ignore old women, Conachar took her advice. One day, as he set out to hunt, the old dog left its place by the hall fire and 'gambolling nimbly as a puppy' accompanied him. At this time the country round was being ravished by an enormous boar. This creature attacked Conachar, his spear and his sword slid off its tough hide and it was his old dog who saved him, killed the boar and was itself killed in the act. Conachar had three sons it is said, John who received land in Aberdeenshire from William the Lion and founded the family of Forbes, Alexander who was sent by the King to Caithness to repel the Danes and whose success was rewarded with their lands after which he founded the family of Mackay, and a third who took the name of Urquhart from the Castle which he inherited. All three were proud to be known as 'Son of the Killer of the Beast' and all adopted a boar's head as their arms in their father's honour. No one seems to have honoured the great hound.

The two strong towers on the landward side of Castle Urquhart were added by Sir William Fitzwarren when he held the castle for Edward I of England during his wars with Scotland. There are many stories of the Castle. Of how the Forbes who held it for Robert the Bruce were starved out by the English troops and how, at the end, they made a last desperate sortie and were all killed. Of how first, however, Forbes' wife, disguised as a serving maid, was allowed safely through the English lines and reached her home in safety, there, in Ireland, to bear his child, and of how later that child regained the Castle. Of how Thomas Randolph, Keeper of the Castle for the Bruce and later guardian of his infant son, King David, administered such justice during the child's minority 'that a man might tie his horse to the Inn rail or leave his plough by the furrow without fear of theft throughout the length and breadth of the land'. His method was simple and direct. He made each sheriff responsible for law and order in his own sheriffdom. If aught was stolen and not recovered, the sheriff must pay its full value out of his own pocket to the bereft owner.

Randolph even stood up to the Pope. A murderer was brought before him in Inverness. He admitted murdering a priest but produced the Pope's absolution—a trick which was growing common. 'The Pope may absolve you from the spiritual consequences of your sin,' said Randolph, 'but of the crime you have committed against the law of this land I am your judge.' The man was executed. But enforcing the law without fear or favour was a dangerous occupation in those days and the 'Good Sir Thomas' was poisoned by 'an infamous friar hired for the purpose'.

There was Lady Mary Ogilvie, the widow of a Laird of Grant, who was Lady of Urquhart and came to a bad end, a refugee, penniless and forlorn, because she refused her support to the Covenanters. Later, there was Mary Grant, daughter of Grant of Castle Urquhart. She loved Donald Donn, the poet son of Macdonald of Bohuntin in Brae Lochaber. Unfortunately Donald looked on cattle lifting as legitimate warfare and the reiver's life as a gentleman's calling. Mary's father did not, and the lovers were forbidden to meet. Nevertheless, meet they did. Donald was an unusual reiver for the place and time, a sort of Robin Hood, killing no one if he could conveniently avoid it and being kind and generous to the poor. It is told of him that one day when driving stolen cattle he saw a strange shadow among them which proved to be an old woman clinging to a cow. He spoke to her and she told him that the cow was hers and all she had. If she lost it she would starve to death, so she might as well die here. 'If you hold like that to one cow what would you do with two?' exclaimed Donald and sent her home with two cows.

One day Donald stopped to see Mary on his way back from a raid. His pursuers were thus able to catch up with the herd he had lifted, though Donald himself escaped. They reported what had happened to the Laird of Grant, who, furious that the stolen cattle had been found on his land, swore to capture and hang Donald. Donald, now well hunted, hid in a cave on the loch-side to be near Mary. His hiding place was discovered and a message, purporting to be from her, was sent to him, entreating him to meet her at the house of a friend. He obeyed and was captured. When Donald had first heard that the Laird of Grant had sworn to hang him he had exclaimed: 'The Devil will take the Laird of Grant out of his shoes and Donald Donn shall not be hanged.' When he was condemned he appealed to be beheaded as a gentleman, not hanged like a felon. This request was granted and he is reputed to have been led away repeating: 'The Devil will take the Laird of Grant out of his shoes and Donald Donn shall not be hanged.' Legend tells how as his severed head rolled from the block it spoke and said: 'Mary lift ye my head.' Some of his poems in Gaelic have survived, including one of which the last verse is:

> Tomorrow I shall be on a hill, without a head.
> Have you no compassion for my sorrowful maiden,
> My Mary, the fair and tender eyed?

The Castle was last occupied by the troops of William of Orange and Mary his Queen. In 1692 they left, blowing up the main fortifications and the towers when they did so. By 1708 all slates and timber had been stolen to build houses, and Castle Urquhart was a ruin as we see it today. Beneath the castle are two huge dungeons. One is filled with treasure, the other with the plague.

The next place of any size is Invermoriston village. Invermoriston House itself was burnt to the ground in 1930. No one ever knew how the fire started, except that it was in the roof. Lightning perhaps. But its gardens and the family burying ground can still be seen between the road and the loch. This was not the first time Invermoriston House was burnt, however. The first stone house on the site was built in the middle of the sixteenth century by a Thane of Cawdor for his much-loved daughter when she married Partick Grant of Glenmoriston. Cawdor is said to have visited the young couple and been horrified to find his daughter living in a wattle house, so, by way of encouraging his son-in-law to allow him to build them a house of stone, he set fire to the old one. No one had seen a stone house in the Glen before and the workmen had all to be brought from Cawdor.

This Patrick Grant was succeeded by his son John, noted for

great size, wit and strength. He visited London in 1631-32 and was much teased as a wild Highlander. One day an acquaintance sneered in his presence at the 'fir candles' of his native glen, 'Glen Moriston the smooth, where the dogs cannot eat the candles'. John bet his tormentor that he could not produce in London a finer candlestick or more brilliant lights than he could bring from his Highland estate. The bet was accepted. 'Glenmoriston' despatched a servant to the North to bring him Iain MacEobhain Bhain, the Glenmoriston bard, noted alike for wit and good looks. At the appointed time the scoffer produced a very fine wrought silver candelabrum holding the best candles. All praised their light. Then, at a signal, the Bard stepped into the chamber in full Highland dress, holding aloft blazing torches cut from the richest pines of Glenmoriston and then steeped in resin. In the blaze of light they produced the candle flames were all but invisible and the astonished spectators adjudged 'Glenmoriston' an easy winner.

Invermoriston House was burnt down yet another time, this time in 1716 by the King's troops as Grant of Glenmoriston was among those who refused to seek pardon and lay down their arms after the Rising.

There are many stories about Invermoriston and the surrounding hills. One tells how a Grant 'of that ilk' had an only and adored son. One day as old Grant sat at breakfast a man in the last stages of exhaustion stumbled into the room, and, grabbing bread and salt from the table, swallowed some, then panted that he was a hunted man and could go no further. He claimed hospitality, the protection of bread and salt. 'I have no choice,' said the Chief, 'you have eaten my bread. Who hunts you and why?' 'I killed a man in a quarrel,' was the answer, 'and his friends are pursuing me.' Grant showed him a safe place to sleep and left him. A few minutes later his pursuers appeared, led, to the horror of the old Chief, by his son's foster-brothers. They told him that his son had been foully murdered and that the murderer, whom they were pursuing, had been seen coming towards the house. 'No one has passed here,' replied the Chief without hesitation, 'try up the Glen.' So they departed and he went to see his son's murderer. He found him sleeping peacefully, unarmed, certain of safety under his enemy's protection. At dusk Grant roused the fugitive, gave him food and wine and bade him go. 'You have till dawn,' he told him, 'then we will hunt and kill you. Go!' And he went.

The old law of hospitality in the Highlands was said to be: 'No guest may be asked his business for one year and one day.' It was also felt that the best must be set before an invited guest. At a dinner given to Argyll by MacEachin in Cantyre the table groaned under one each of every available creature, roasted whole and set on the table 'standing on its stumps'. Ox, goat, sheep, stag, roe, hares, rabbits and innumerable varieties of poultry were said to have been so displayed.

A road to the West takes off from Invermoriston and runs through Glenmoriston, Glenshiel and Kintail to the western sea and Kyle of Lochalsh. Six miles further along the main road from Invermoriston is Fort Augustus, at the head of the Loch, where the road from the Loch's southern shore joins it and where there is also a fine 'stair' of locks connecting the Loch with the next stretch of the canal. Fort Augustus was so named by General Wade about 1730 in honour of His Royal Highness William Augustus, Duke of Cumberland, better known in the North as Stinking Willie and Butcher Cumberland. The old Gaelic name for the village was Cilchumen (or Kiltcheumein), the Church of Cummin, St. Cummein the Fair who wrote a biography of St. Columba about 650 being the saint in question.

The story goes that St. Cummein founded an abbey or some form of religious house here long before the present Benedictine abbey was born or thought of. The country round was wild and uncultivated and the saint, seeing the need both to grow grain for the making of meal and also to spread knowledge of agriculture among the primitive inhabitants, bade his monks clear and plough a parcel of land round their holy house. At first all went well but it was desperately hard work and some of the monks began to grumble. It was for them to lead a leisured life teaching and preaching, they said; let others clear the ground and plough. God could not mean *them* to do it. At last matters came to a head and one monk, bolder than the rest, faced the saint and told him that if God had need of ploughed land He must provide it; they would not. 'So be it, my son,' replied the saint, 'but you may not eat of the fruits thereof', and he went to his cell to pray while the monks, half joyful, half fearful, took a holiday and went fishing. When they rose next morning, rather late for none had rung the abbot's bell, they saw the saint standing by the disputed land and talking to a team of red deer harnessed to the monks' plough. Already some land was ploughed. All day the deer ploughed and the saint watched. Frightened and shamefaced, the monks did their daily tasks and brought food to the saint, who refused it, and fodder to the stags, who ate daintily. As evening fell, the saint stopped the tired beasts and, thanking them for their work, for they had done much, sent them back to their hills with his blessing. That night two monks arose and went quietly out to see the deer's furrows. It was their intention to plough till dawn now that they knew it to be the will of God. But the plough was gone from its shed by the water's edge and there, ploughing at speed in the quiet moonlight, was an enormous black stallion, the waterhorse of Loch Ness. By dawn all the land lay ploughed in the sun's rays and the great horse had returned to his own place, but on his back had gone a rider, the monk who tried to teach the Lord.

It is interesting to note in this old story that even from the beginning the Iona Church tried to teach agriculture and civilised ways to a very primitive and backward people. Later, improving education and way of life was one of their great tasks. Another was the encouraging of all men to come and pray in the tiny churches at any time they felt the desire, that they might learn for themselves the power of prayer. This was one of the main differences between Celtic and Roman Churches in the early days in the Highlands. The Roman Catholic priests held prayer in their own hands to a far greater extent, the Celtic Church held it out as God's gift to every man.

The second of the Great Glen roads runs along the south shore of Loch Ness. Leaving Inverness at the foot of Bridge Street it passes the War Memorial and the Islands and then runs parallel with the River Ness almost as far as the village of Dores. On the left a few miles from Inverness is Ness Castle, at the moment a hotel. Of it McBain in his *Place Names* says its 'old name was Borlum, meaning Bordlands, whence the infamous and notorious

Borlum family got its name'. It would be interesting to know what this 'infamous' family was and what it did. Unfortunately it seems to be no longer notorious. Next comes Aldourie, now turned into flats, with a lovely position on the Loch, and then, about a mile further on, the village of Dores, before we reach which there is a fine view down the length of Loch Ness. The chief claim of Dores to fame today is that her inn is kept by a retired lady's maid of the Queen Mother.

> If you'd seen this road
> Before it was made
> You'd hold up your hand
> And bless General Wade.

Few truer rhymes have ever been remembered, for General Wade made the first road through the Great Glen, *circa* 1726, where this one now runs. His reputation for fair dealing, justice and hard work remains a very live memory, as do the many roads he made, most of which, like this one, are still in use. It was down this road that Johnson and Boswell travelled and Dr Johnson much admired the Loch, adding two pieces of information about it that he obtained at Fort Augustus. One was that 'its water is imagined by the natives to be medicinal', an idea long since extinct, and the other that it was said to remain open in the hardest winters. It is certainly a fact that I have seen the Beauly Firth frozen almost across and the Cromarty Firth completely frozen and able to bear a cart, both of these being salt-water lochs, when Loch Ness had only a little thin ice round the shore. Whether it ever has been known to freeze, however, I don't know.

Beyond Dores the road becomes unimaginably beautiful, both for scenery and for the more homely things such as birch woods yellow with primroses, the young green of the birches themselves, the flaming scarlet of rowan trees standing out amid the guinea gold of birches in autumn, warm old gold of oak woods studded here and there with the living green of firs, and, loveliest of all, in the winter the birches again, grey and purple against the snow. In the woods on this side of the Loch there were once herds of wild horses, creatures rather of the hill pony type; shaggy and sure-footed, they roamed about the hills from Moray to Sutherland but these woods were one of their favourite haunts. In the

Loch Ness

woods, too, was an enormous yellow horse, some say more than one, who carried off boys and young men. Two young brothers once went to fish in Loch Ness. Before they set out their father warned them to beware of 'the Horse'. Sure enough, the horse came down to the loch-side to drink and both boys were overwhelmed with admiration for its beauty. Never before had they seen such a stallion. Its coat glowed like some fine silk cloth, finer than either boy had ever imagined, its mane was like the silken floss of a maiden's hair and its eyes were sad. Surely so fine a creature could not be evil. The boys did not try to escape and when it approached and offered them a ride the elder boy could not resist. He sprang on its back and instantly found himself glued on, unable to move. He tried to cry a warning to his young brother, but too late; the boy had raised his hand to stroke the arching neck and as he touched the glossy skin his hand stuck fast. Realising their danger, the younger boy drew his knife and cut off his own fingers, then, as at sight of steel the horse fled, bound up his hand with the healing leaves of figwort and followed its track through the woods, stopping only as he passed their home to take his brother's sword. All day he followed the horse's track and just as night fell he came upon it resting by a burn, his brother still fast on its back. Creeping up, the boy lifted the sword and managed to cut off the beautiful golden head. To his amazement, he had hardly done so when there stood before him not only his brother freed from the spell but another and very handsome young man with white skin and golden hair. In his hand the youth held the boy's fingers. 'How can I thank you for freeing me?' he asked, adding, 'Show me your hand.' The boy removed the bandage and the youth replaced his fingers and his hand grew whole once more. The golden youth told them of how he had fallen under the spell of a magician which could only be broken if his head was cut off by one who had never before held a sword. The three young men strolled happily home together but the brothers were lucky, for many a boy or man who met a yellow horse was never seen again.

The black stallion of Loch Ness and the yellow horses of the woods were not the only equine inhabitants of the Great Glen. There was also the White Mare of Corri-Dho, who dwelt in the hills between Glenmoriston and Glen Urquhart. She was a creature of such overwhelming charm that no horse could resist her. Any horse turned out to graze anywhere in the Great Glen would immediately seek her and would never be seen again. At last the men of the district determined to intervene. They made a cordon round her in her favourite haunt and slowly the lines drew closer till it seemed that she could not escape. But one of them, Alexander Cutach (or the Short), conceited as small men so often are, thought he could capture the beauty single-handed and seized her by the tail. Infuriated, she broke through the cordon with Alexander attached, for his hand was stuck fast. Later, his mangled body was found on the moor, but of the White Mare there was no trace; she had returned to wherever she belonged.

Close to Dores village three large stones can be seen in the waters of the loch. The centre one of these is known as 'The Thieves' Stone' because cattle raiders could tell by the height of the water on its side whether or not the 'lifted' cattle could safely cross the ford at Bona. A little farther along the road is the Well of the Outstretched Hand which was said to be the abode of some large-sized spirit whose phantom hand would often be seen stretched out over the heads of those about to drink the well water. Many thirsty travellers were terrified but I never heard of one being harmed and no one seems to know the origin or purpose of the apparition. The well was marked with a name stone in 1922. A little farther yet on the road is a crossing of a deep burn on whose banks two fugitives from Culloden died of their wounds and a stone carved with the date 1746 can still be found in the ravine. Burns, big and small, are almost as plentiful as corners on this road and near the next bridge, the witch's bridge, there lived a witch with a very evil eye as late as 1881 when she invited herself, like the witches in the fairy tales, to the wedding of the then Fraser Tytler of Aldourie, bringing with her, in a cooking pot, a highly magic potion of a gruel-like nature.

Further on again we pass the site of General Wade's camp and later, near a small piece of arable land, are the outlines of an ancient cottage. Here a tiny 'change house' or posting inn stood at the time of Culloden. Its owner had recently died and the inn was in the hands of his old and crippled mother and pretty young daughter. One of Cumberland's officers saw and admired the girl and assaulted her. The old grandmother tried to protect her, whereupon the officer throttled the old woman in her chair and turned once more to the girl. But she had used the moment to escape and made her way to a settlement known as 'the town of the freebooters' on the loch side. The men of the township returned with her, made the officer a prisoner and took both him and the old woman's body to the Duke at Fort Augustus. He expressed anger and ordered the officer to 'mend his manners and pay blood money'. It was at this same cottage that Dr Johnson and Mr Boswell called and were surprised to find an old woman alone in the house and obviously afraid of them. But the inn was not, perhaps, as innocent as it appeared, for a little later the paymaster of the troops at Fort Augustus stopped there for the night after a visit to Inverness to collect a large bag of gold coin. Neither he nor his horse, its harness or the gold were ever seen again. Some claimed that he was murdered and his body thrown into Loch Ness, others that this was what he wished to be believed.

The next point of interest is where the road to Inverfarigaig takes off to the left, with its precipitous river valley and its slopes starry with grass of Parnassus and scabious. This is not a road to take lightly; to get round the bend into it many cars must reverse. However, one gets good warning for the start of the road is an avenue of cypress-like trees. Not far from the Inverfarigaig turning comes the pleasant little Foyers Hotel and then Foyers itself with its Falls, its aluminium works and its monster, for the favourite sporting ground of 'Nessie' lies between Foyers and Fort Augustus. Foyers had the honour of being bombed in the war, not by mistake but of intent.

Beyond Foyers lies Camus Mharbh Dhaoine, The Bay of the Dead Men, so called because of a fierce fight there between the galleys of Portclair (who had come to avenge a slight to his young bride) and the men of Grant who rowed out to meet him. Needless to say, the galleys defeated the small boats with much slaughter and the Grants lost Foyers. But who Gruer Mor of Portclair was and how or why his bride was slighted in Foyers I should hate to guess. What was she doing in Foyers anyway?

Portclair is on the other shore. Traditionally she came there to collect bride gifts, but this seems a little unusual.

From there the road runs on, beautifully, down to Fort Augustus.

FORT AUGUSTUS
TO BALLACHULISH

Bannocks o' bear meal,
Bannocks o' barley,
Here's to the Highlandman's
Bannocks o' barley.

ROBERT BURNS

AFTER FORT AUGUSTUS the road follows the line of the Canal and the shores of Loch Oich and Loch Lochy to Fort William. It first passes through some flat land, probably once water meadows, which has always been a popular gathering place for the clans and camping place of armies. There are not, when you look around, very many possible camping grounds to be found in this part of the Highlands; the high ground is too high and the low too marshy. It was here that the Earls of Mar and of Caithness camped with the troops of King James I of Scotland before the fatal battle of Inverlochy, when Caithness was killed on the field and Mar escaped alone and on foot into the Great Glen. The Highlanders had won a signal victory. Severely wounded, Mar wandered in the hills till at last he was saved by a herd-woman who found him dying of hunger and exhaustion. Having neither cup nor platter, she took off his shoe, mixed barley meal and water in it and gave it to him. Later he composed a verse in Gaelic of which the following is a translation:

Hunger is a cook right good
Woe to him that sneers at food—
Barley crowdie in my shoe
The sweetest food I ever knew.

Another army to camp here was that of Claverhouse, 'Bonny Dundee'. He was more fortunate than the two earls for he left it to win a noted victory, the Battle of Killiecrankie. Among others with him was Lochiel, who was credited with possessing

37

second sight. Before the battle Dundee enquired from him which side would be victorious and he replied 'the Army which first sheds blood'. The two armies were already drawn up facing one another and Locheil's words ran like wildfire through the troops till they reached young Grant of Glenmoriston who called an accomplished Glenmoriston deer-stalker to him, repeated the prophecy and at the same time pointed out an officer mounted on a white horse in front of the enemy's lines as being 'most conspicuous'. The stalker took aim and ensured victory for Dundee. General Monk passed here too, en route for Glengarry, but he is reputed not to have camped; only delayed long enough to burn all the houses of Glen Roy. The Duke of Cumberland spent seven weeks in Fort Augustus, itself a misfortune for any district.

Little Loch Oich is the first in the chain of lochs after Loch Ness. It is a slim, narrow piece of water between high fir-covered hillsides, very attractive but not unsuited to its name if, as some say, it means The Place of Awe. Long before 'Nessie' stole the limelight Loch Oich had its own monster, a waterhorse with a difference, for its head was said to be flat rather than horse-shaped; it took no interest in human beings but was reputed to watch for sheep or deer coming to drink from the loch; these it would seize and, dragging them into the water, sit on their heads until they drowned. Some claimed to have seen the creature behaving as described; others, however, held that she was too convenient an alibi for deer poachers and sheep stealers to be entirely credible, especially as sheep do not drink. Also, her manner of killing was queer. Actually, I once knew a dog, an elderly spaniel, who did just that. He would drive his master's sheep, one at a time, into the sea and then, deliberately and of malice aforethought, sit on its head till it died. At that point he would lose all interest in it, come quietly ashore and start again with another one.

On the north shore of Loch Oich stand the ruins of the old Macdonald Castle of Glengarry, three times burnt. The huge Macdonald Clan, with its many leading families, has a queer history of marriage and inter-marriage, even marriage in Scotland not recognised in England and vice-versa. At last their descents became such a tangle that a case was brought before the House of Lords, that the Law Lords might sift the evidence and decide who was in fact the Chief of the Clan. The House did its best but had finally to decide that on present evidence no decision was possible as between the three leading families, Clanranald, Glengarry and Sleat, and that they could only suggest that these three take the Chieftainship in rotation. The history and adventures of Clan Donald would fill many tomes but on one thing all are agreed—Macdonald pride. Once, it is said, a woman in Lochaber went to Confession and admitted that her besetting sin was pride. The priest reproved her for it and gave her advice on how to subdue it. She listened reverently and then said: 'God and men know I have a right to be proud. I was born a Macdonald.'

Once Glengarry House, which stands not far from the ruins of the Castle, had a brownie but the unfortunate little creature was accidentally scalded while helping in the kitchen. He promptly left, taking, it is believed, the luck of the house with him. The road to the West by Glengarry and Tomdoun takes off to the right here and nearby is the famous Well of the Heads, where Iain Lom, the Gaelic Poet Laureate to Charles II, washed the heads of the seven murderers of Macdonald of Keppoch before presenting them to 'Glengarry'. He is said to have carried them on his saddle bow, strung together by a withy through their ears. An odd way for a poet to behave, perhaps, but he was of the Keppoch family and felt strongly on clan matters, as some of his verses show. For instance:

> Up the green slope of Cuil-Eachhaidh
> Came Clan Donald, marching stoutly;
> Churls who laid my home in ashes
> Now shall pay the fine devoutly.
>
>   *   *   *   *   *
>
> On the wings of eager rumour
> Far and wide the tale is flying,
> How the slippery knaves, the Campbells,
> With their cloven skulls are lying.'
> (From his 'Battle of Inverlochy')

After Loch Oich comes Loch Lochy, the home of a water goddess and, most strange to relate, she is black. All this was St. Finan's country and he had once a small church near the loch, presumably to control her. The hillsides beside the loch have been forested, with excellent results. The road is now almost always usable whereas in the years before the planting heavy rain, snow and frost were all liable to bring down a landslide of loose stone and shale, burying the roadway. I can remember in 1922 or 1923 my father's car being caught between two such falls. We got out by driving along the loch's narrow and stony beach with two wheels in the water part of the way. The result was four punctures and one broken spring, but we got through.

Not far to the north-west of this loch lies Loch Arkaig where it has long been believed Prince Charles's French treasure was hidden. Its exact whereabouts (if it really existed) are not known and though many have searched no trace has ever been found. By tradition three men knew the secret and all died without revealing it.

With Loch Lochy the 'real' lochs end and the road rises over some higher ground between it and the sea-loch, Loch Linnhe, on which Fort William stands. The Canal, too, crosses the high ground to Banavie by the Giant's Staircase (also called Neptune's Staircase), a very fine sequence of locks but uneconomical in use. In the days when MacBrayne's ran a steamer service between Inverness and Oban, one steamer stopped below the locks and another took on at Fort William, the connecting link being supplied by a bus. The road from Loch Lochy by Spean Bridge to Fort William runs by moor and riverside. It is a lonely, rather bare country full of sad tales and much overshadowed by the enormous bulk of Ben Nevis looking squarely down on it all. It was here that in the last war most of our Commando troops were trained. A striking monument to them has been erected in a dominating position hard by the road. Much of this Glen became the Great Glen Cattle Ranch, where great herds wander over the hills. It was a pioneer scheme and may do much for the Highlands. The original owners of the Ranch are now the owners of the present Inverlochy Castle where Queen Victoria once stayed. The old Castle of Inverlochy was in its heyday the palace of the Kings of Scots and is supposed to date from A.D. 600 or 700.

Once a Glaistic (a sort of fairy woman) inhabited the slopes above Inverlochy. She was up to many a trick and her presence was not at all popular with the local people. One day Big

The Commando Monument

Kennedy of Lianachan saw her near his farm and managed to seize her. He heated a ploughshare red hot, then let it cool to black and said to her: 'If you will swear on this ploughshare that you will trouble the people of the Glen no more, I will set you free.' The Glaistic placed 'her lovely little hand' on the ploughshare and it was burnt to the bone. She fled screaming up the hillside and there 'the blood of her heart burst forth' and she died. As she was dying she said:

> Growth like fern to them
> Wasting like rushes to them,
> And as unlasting as the mist of the hill.

and that curse has been on Big Kennedy's descendants ever since, while the vegetation round the spot where she died is still russet hued, stained by her heart's blood.

One of the stories told of this bleak moor is of a party of soldiers, who, marching back to Fort Augustus after the massacre of Glencoe, heard the sound of piping in the hills. Believing that a Macdonald piper must have been among those who had escaped the massacre and that he was now using his pipes to collect stragglers, the officer in charge ordered his men on to the moor in search of him. The piping soon grew louder and clearer but ever kept ahead of them until at last the music led the party to a small hill loch and vanished into the water. It was a piper of the Little People that they followed and he gladly led them astray. Hungry, footsore and angry, the party began their struggle back through the snow to the valley below. As they went, another sound broke the stillness of the snow-clad hills—the crying of a young child. The officer called up one of his men. 'Find that child and wring its neck,' he ordered angrily, 'then follow our tracks down.' The soldier went off as bidden, with as bad a grace as he dared, for he too was tired and hungry. Led by the baby's crying he began to climb again. Then the sound stopped. Instead came the loveliest singing he had ever heard. Soon he came upon the singer. It was a young mother, an escaped fugitive, utterly exhausted, lulling her baby to the sleep of death in the snow. When she saw the soldier, sword in hand, she did not move. She was too tired. He looked down at mother and child but could not speak to them for they had no English and he no Gaelic. But he remembered how he had left his own wife with their baby in her arms, took what little food he had and offered it to the woman, then took off his greatcoat to wrap round the child. Then he turned and ran. On his way down he passed another woman who had also escaped the massacre but this one was less fortunate; the wolf that had killed her was still at his feast. The soldier slew the wolf and when he rejoined his party and was asked by the officer: 'Did you get the child?', replied: 'I found it' and held up his sword, stained with the wolf's blood. The officer grunted and the party marched on. It is pleasant to know that the woman and child survived and their descendants are said to be in Lochaber today.

This same moor was once the favourite hunting ground of a young hunter, Donald Cameron. One day he shot at a hind and wounded it but though he followed her for some time the deer escaped. Months later Donald was overtaken by darkness and decided to spend the night on the moor. He found shelter beneath a boulder and soon fell asleep, but his sleep was disturbed by the appearance of a most beautiful woman who approached him and offered him an arrow. 'Never did I believe you would harm me, Donald,' she said reproachfully, 'after the many hours we have wandered together over the hill.' 'But,' said the perplexed Donald, 'I never saw you before and I certainly never harmed you or any woman, and where did you get my arrow?' 'I am the hind you shot with this arrow,' she answered. 'I am the leader of my herd and many a happy day on the hill have I led you to. I am under Fith Fath (enchantment).' The young man did not know what to do at all but accepted the arrow and promised in future only to shoot at stags, not hinds. Then the maiden moved away with her deer and he heard her singing:

> I would not let my herd of deer,
> My herd of deer, my herd of deer,
> I would not let my herd of deer
> Go seek grey shells upon the strand.
>
> They had rather the cresses green,
> The cresses green, the cresses green,
> They had rather the cresses green
> That grow on the mead of the glorious springs.

Slowly the singing died away among the hills.

A mile or two before Fort William is reached a road takes off to Banavie (the Canal mouth) and Corpach, the Place of Bodies. This name goes back to the days when kings and chiefs were taken to Iona for burial. If, as frequently happened, the sea was not calm enough for the funeral barge to sail, the whole party remained with the body at Corpach until it was safe to set out. Funerals to Iona went in great state.

And this is the manner in which a Lord of the Isles would die. His fair body was brought to Iona of Colum-cille. And the Abbot and the monks and the vicars came forth to meet the King of the Isles; and his service and waking were honourably performed during eight days and eight nights; after which his full, noble body was laid in the same grave with his fathers, in the Reilig of Oran.

This account is of the burying of Donald, King of the Isles, who received his Sceptre of the Isles from his brother Ranald. 'He was the son of Good John, son of Angus Og, son of Angus Mor, son of Donald, son of Ranald, son of Somerled, the noble and renowned High Chief of the Hebrides.' He made a reliquary or covering of gold and silver for the hand of St. Columba.

To this day lights are seen on the waters of Loch Leven, shimmering where the funeral barges passed carrying Kings and Chiefs to their burial.

St. Columba and his monks often visited this part of the mainland and it was said to be near here that St. Columba was once approached by a beggar. The Saint did not approve of begging and said so in no uncertain terms. The man explained that he was a hunter to trade but such a bad one that he was rarely successful and now that he was too weak from hunger to follow the deer on the hills his wife and children would starve. St. Columba then took pity on him and gave him a 'blessed pike' which would hunt for him by killing any animal at which it was pointed. The man went home happy and soon he and his family were sleek and well-liking, with open door for every neighbour. But the day came when Columba returned to the district and found the man again a beggar. He explained that his wife had taken a dislike to the blessed pike, fearing it might harm the children, and had made him destroy it.

Near Loch Eil, at the head of Loch Linnhe, lived a poor man who once gave St. Columba a night's hospitality. In the morning the Saint asked him how many cows he had. 'Five,' was the reply. 'A hundred and five they shall become, neither more nor less, answered the Saint, and so it came to pass. No matter how many he used or gave to the needy, his herd grew no less, and no matter how hard he tried to increase the number his herd grew no larger.

Fort William itself was built close to the village of Auchintore and was called after William of Orange, while the village had its name changed to Maryburgh in honour of Mary his wife. Later, both names were changed to Gordonsburgh by a Duke of Gordon who did not love the House of Orange, and later again, with the 'passing' of the Gordons, it became Duncanburgh to please Sir Duncan Cameron of Fossfearn who had no love for the House of Gordon. Now, and one hopes finally, it has reverted to being Fort William.

Beyond Fort William the road follows the lochside through

Onich to North Ballachulish and the ferry to Argyll, or round Loch Leven on the Inverness-shire shore to Kinlochleven with its aluminium works. A most lovely drive. Once Sir Ewen Cameron of Locheil was going along the ferry road in peace when he was overtaken by a noted witch, Great Gormul of Moy, who had followed him all the way from Inverness.

'Step on, beloved Ewen,' she greeted him, but he, knowing well that she did not love him, answered,

'Step on thyself, Carlin. And if it be necessary to take the step, a step beyond thee for Ewen.'

'Step on, beloved Ewen,' she said again, and he answered much as before,

'Step to step with thee, old one, and the odd step to Ewen.'

And so they went on down to the loch shore. When they reached the ferry Sir Ewen was still one step ahead. He hailed the ferry and stepped quickly on board. Great Gormul made to follow him but the ferryman, knowing who she was, would not take her. Then she said farewell to Sir Ewen, adding, 'And the wish of my heart to thee, thou best beloved of men, Ewen.'

'The wish of thy heart be upon yonder grey stone, Carlin,' he retorted. And instantly the stone split in two.

GLEN URQUHART

Gloom and silence and spell,
Spell and silence and gloom,
And the weird death-light burns dim in the night
And the dead men rise from the tomb.
                    MURDOCH MACLEAN

GLEN URQUHART is the only place I ever heard of that recognises three Devils, the Black Devil, the Speckled Devil and the White Devil, and the last of these three, because he was able to assume the appearance of an angel or other good spirit and so deceive men, was by far the most deadly.

Glen Urquhart first appears in written history in Adamnan's *Life of St. Columba*. Once, while the saint and his monks were journeying down Loch Ness, it was revealed to St. Columba that he must hurry to Glen Urquhart (Airchart-Dan) where he would find an old man named Emchath on his death-bed and should baptise him. 'For he is a man who has always preserved his natural goodness and angels are already on their way for his soul.' St. Columba did as directed and duly found Emchath. The saint preached the word of God to him and he believed and was baptised, then 'safe and joyfully with the angels who met him he passed away to the Lord'.

A somewhat similar summons came to one of the 'Men' as Glen Urquhart called certain virtuous Elders, many centuries later. He too was summoned to a dying man to pray with him. It was a dark and stormy night when, wrapping himself in a cloak, he set out. As he passed along the wooded bank of the Meiklie Burn he heard a whimpering and found a baby lying under a bush, cold and wet. Wrapping the shivering child in his cloak he hoisted it on to his back and continued his way, but the child grew heavier and heavier until at last he felt he must rest. When he would have risen again to go on he found himself being held down by a hideous monster whose horrible hairy hands were already round his neck. He fought fiercely to free himself, then, realising it must be a creature of evil, he called aloud on God for help and the creature—who is believed to have been undoubtedly the White Devil—disappeared, leaving him free to visit and pray with the dying man, which obviously it had hoped to prevent.

Glen Urquhart is the only district, too, where as far as I know, the Devil in person has beaten and kicked men to death. In other places he is content to incite others to such deeds. It is, I believe, usually the Speckled Devil who behaves in this manner. But the power of evil in this Glen has always seemed stronger and a more sentient thing than anywhere else in Scotland. It is a glen both larger and longer than it appears at its mouth; now a route which even tour buses take, it was until well into this century completely remote. No public transport of any sort connected it with the outside world until the 1920's. The consequence was that the Glen was famed alike for its Gaelic (Glen Urquhart Gaelic was said to be the purest in Scotland) and for its witches—real 'black' ones. When Gaelic came from Ireland to Scotland it naturally changed considerably over the ages till now a man speaking Erse and one speaking Gaelic have considerable difficulty in understanding one another. But Gaelic in Scotland itself also changed very much in different districts. In the time of St. Columba and his Church it was the language in which his monks preached, so it slowly ousted the old Pictish tongue and became universal in the Highlands. But geographical features such as sea and mountains separated the different localities, as also did such long-lasting Clan feuds as that between the Campbells of Argyll and the Macdonalds of the Isles, with the result that various dialects of Gaelic grew up in different places, differing greatly, and each claiming itself to be the true Gaelic. Finally they have boiled down to three: Argyllshire Gaelic which is the best known and the one most closely akin to Erse, containing many Irish words and forms I am told; Island Gaelic, to some extent contaminated by Norse words and forms of speech; and Glen Urquhart Gaelic, said to be the purest of them all. No doubt B.B.C. Gaelic will soon supplant all three.

Witches are a different matter. As a child I used to stay with an aunt at Kilmartin on Loch Meiklie, well up the Glen. In those days there was no public transport at all. Letters for the 'Big Houses' were sent out by horse from Inverness in locked letter bags, one bag for each house. Each owner had his key, emptied out the incoming post and replaced it with the outgoing mail, if any, and that was that. My cousin had many small friends round about who showed us birds' nests and other joys. One day, two of them told me they had something special to show me—my cousin, being older, was still at lessons—and took me to a little burn which came tumbling down the hillside not far from Hazel Brae. Here, hidden and held fast by two stones, was a queer little wax doll. It had a few strands of real hair on its head, nail parings stood out like fingers from the ends of its arms, its eyes were tiny bits of coal, horribly shiny and alive-looking. 'Don't touch; it might do things,' I was warned. I didn't understand, but in some queer way I was very frightened, not so much of the image as of the whole feel of things. Perhaps the other children were frightened (they were certainly awed) and this frightened me. One of them told me who had made the image and whose image it was, and explained that the woman in question was a witch. If a witch made an image and put it in the burn, the burn would wear it away very slowly but surely, and the man whose image it was would equally slowly but surely die. Anyone could make an image but only a witch knew the proper things to say to it. They had found this one because they had seen the farmer whose image it was, turning the witch's cows out of his corn and so they were sure she would make an image of him and he would die. All this was explained by the same child who had explained butter-making to me a few days before, and in the same matter-of-fact tone, and I found it much the more natural and the easier to believe of the two. After all, why *should* milk turn into butter? Or, for that matter, why should anyone in love entering the dairy disturb the butter and prevent its 'coming' as I was told it did?

Needless to say, I was sworn to secrecy and we waited for what we regarded as the certain result. Then I went home and soon forgot, till my aunt came to stay a few months later and mentioned in my hearing how sorry she was for this farmer's wife and children as he had just died, quite young. The doctors did not know why or of what. I kept the secret for many years and with it a fear and horror of witchcraft. Even yet I sometimes wonder whether evil and hatred let loose by anyone in any concentrated form such as 'over-looking' or cursing may not do harm beyond our comprehension, just as blessings may do good.

Some years later my mother engaged that witch's daughter as housemaid, and a very good and well trained one she was. At first all went well, her work was well done, she was tidy and pleasant, but on several occasions my mother found the other maids doing things which were her work; however, a kitchen in which one obliges another (within limits) is usually a happy kitchen. But one winter morning my mother, taking a short cut down the back stairs, came upon a procession. In front walked Peggy, a lady of leisure; behind her came the tablemaid with brush and dustpan; last but not least came Cook in person, carrying kindling for the fires. The resultant enquiries elicited the fact that Peggy did not like to spoil her hands doing grates or dusting, nor did she like to tire herself with a broom, and: 'We wouldn't wish to offend her mother so we just do it ourselves. . . . Oh, no, M'm, please you mustn't say anything. We couldn't stay if you did. Indeed we wouldn't be safe from bad luck *anywhere* if her mother thought we had grudged the work or complained. . . . No, you *can't* make a change, M'm, anything might happen.' Having satisfied herself that nothing would be done which could offend Peggy's redoubtable mother, Cook, who belonged to an older generation and had been a noted player of the 'proverb game' in the Ceilidhs of her youth, added with scorn: 'But the laziness of her! Yon would be "a good messenger to send for death", but there, "Clean bird never left kite's nest." '

In the end, as my mother saw no point in paying Peggy for doing practically nothing, and as it was obvious that no one local would dare to come to us if we contrived to annoy Peggy's mother, we had to close the house for a time, dismiss the whole staff (officially) and start fresh on our return. 'I could wait and come back to you,' Peggy offered when she heard, and it was felt it would be tactless to reply: 'No, thank you, we don't believe in witches but we won't re-engage a witch's child.'

Between the wars a Yorkshire man who had bought a place

in the Glen decided to rear pigs and brought up his pig-man from Yorkshire to superintend. This swineherd quarrelled with a woman in the Glen reputed to be the possessor of the Evil Eye. She was seen to walk past the piggeries and eighty-three young pigs were dead next day. 'Over-looking' said everyone, including (it was believed) the young and rather scared policeman. But the owner himself said: 'Poison', and announced that if any more of his animals died he would call in Scotland Yard. No more died.

The Little People lived in Glen Urquhart also. An Gobha Mor —the Big Smith or Armourer—knew all about that. He and his seven sons were noted alike in their day for their strength and their skill. The fame of their cold-iron swords spread throughout Scotland. In making these much-prized weapons the iron was heated and shaped by heavy and repeated hammer blows, without the use of fire. The smith's herd of cattle on his farm at Polmaily were also famous for their perfections. One morning the smith, visiting his byre, found his cattle looking lean and hungry and no matter what he did they grew scraggier and scraggier. Near Polmaily was the fairy hillock of Tornashee and one of the fairies from it was the smith's 'fairy-love', a relationship not very uncommon in those parts in his time. She told him the fairies had carried off and eaten his cattle. Furious, he took his axe and rushed to the byre to kill the fairy kine, but when they saw him coming they all slipped their heads out of their head-ropes and escaped. The smith caught the last by its tail and was carried with it, willy nilly, over grassland and moorland, over bog and rock, till they came to Carn-an-Rath in Ben-an Gharbhlaich near Achnababan. As they approached this hill or dun it opened to admit them. No sooner were they within than the cattle turned back into some of the Little People. The smith, looking round, found himself in a fine hall, full of rare jewels, gold and silver. The fairy chief politely apologised for his rough ride and also for 'lifting' his cattle and asked him to take any one thing he saw as recompense. Many of the fine jewels were of far greater value than his herd but the smith noticed in a far corner a small shaggy pony and, remembering something his fairy-love had once told him of the powers and strength of this horse, he avoided the jewels (which would most likely have turned to dead leaves

50

anyway) and chose the filly. 'A tooth out of your informant's mouth' cried the angry Little People but they gave him the pony, only warning him never to harness it to anything but the plough,

Highland Ponies in snow

and let him go. Wise indeed was his choice, for never so strong a horse was seen in the Highlands.

> Achnababan she could plough,
> And Lurgamore from east to west
> Likewise Gorstan-Keppagach
> And still plough on without a rest.

But one day the smith harnessed her to a cart and her powers left her.

Once the Urquhart men drove their cattle to feed in Corri Dho, but two supernatural beings there drove them out, crying:

> Mine are Doire-Dhamb and Doire-Dhailbhidh
> And yellow Borrisgidh of the streams
> And wide Ceanacroc, with its woods and pasturage.
> Ye black and singed carles, take yourselves away.

Glen Urquhart was the scene of many a Clan fight and many a cattle-lifting and its consequences. There is hardly a stone or a hollow that is not known by some such name as 'The Hollow of the Dead Men', 'The Stone of the Slaying' and so on. But despite the horror of its past it is a very beautiful valley, especially perhaps in winter with its birches purple against the snow, Loch Meiklie reflecting the cold clear blue of the sky and Corrimony woods white with the white purity of snowdrops. It looks more a country for angels than witches and wars. Yet it is close to these very woods that those with 'the sight' may receive warning of horrors to come, in the form of vast shadowy hosts battling over the Corrimony moors. What their coming portends no man knows, except that it is a sight of unimaginable evil.

The road crosses Corrimony and runs over the moors and then down a steep hill with beautiful views to the River Cannich. To go by Glen Urquhart to Glen Affric, returning by way of Glen Cannich and Chisholm's Tooth, makes a most memorable drive. It is not quite so good if done in reverse as one then misses the views running down the long hill from Glen Urquhart to Cannich.

Between Corrimony and Invermoriston lies a piece of very wild country once occupied by a Cailleach a'Chrathaich or Hag of the Cràach as that part was called. She had a grievance against the MacMillans and used to accost every wayfarer to discover his name and, if it was MacMillan, engage his attention in the most pleasing manner and quietly steal his bonnet and then leave him. She would seat herself and begin to rub the bonnet between two stones—as it wore thin the man began to tire and when at length a hole came he dropped down dead. Once Donald MacMillan of Balmacaan saw her steal his cap, a fierce struggle ensued, he escaped with it unharmed, but as he went she hissed after him that he would die at nine of the clock three nights thence. As the clock struck the fatal hour he fell back in his chair dead. Not far off, near Tornashee, lived a good and gentle spirit who did what she could to warn and protect travellers from the Hag. She had a passion for riding and once asked Donald Macrae of Lochletter for a lift. He placed her before him on his horse then, binding her with the horse rope, took her home a prisoner and tied her to his door-post. Instantly the place was surrounded by crowds of furious Little People who, shouting and screaming curses upon him, stripped the building of every bit of roof. Thoroughly frightened, Macrae offered to let her go if she would rebuild his house. To this she agreed and called:

> Speed wood and sod
> To the house of Macrae
> Except honeysuckle and bird-cherry.

Instantly, timber and turf came flying in through the air and soon the house was restored as it had been and the good fairy was freed. Macrae had better luck than he deserved that time.

GLENMORISTON
AND GLENGARRY

O'er the moor at midnight
The wee folk pass,
They whisper 'mong the rushes
And o'er the green grass;
All through the marshy places
They glint and pass away,
The light folk, the lone folk
the folk that will not stay.

*   *   *   *   *

O never wrong the wee folk,
The red folk and the green,
The fierce folk, the angry folk,
the folk that steal and slay.
DONALD A. MACKENZIE

THE MAIN ROAD to Glenelg, Lochalsh and Skye, when it turns off the Loch Ness road, first runs beside the River Moriston. Moriston is said to come from an old Pictish word meaning waterfall, and certainly for many centuries Glenmoriston Falls were worthy of note. They are beautiful even now, though two hydro-electric dams between them and Loch Cluanie have greatly reduced their perfection.

Glenmoriston has always been a main route to the West and tradition speaks of the Lords of the Isles and other important chiefs passing through it with considerable pomp. A number of Macdonalds had once settled here and it is said that whenever Macdonald of the Isles passed through 'in state' he formally exchanged shirts with the chief of the Glenmoriston Macdonalds as a pledge of 'mutual friendship and fidelity'. There were five septs of these Macdonalds in Glenmoriston and four of them were descended from four sons of Iain Mor Ruigh-nan-Stop (Great

Iain of the Liquor-Pot!). Iain Mor had sixteen fine sons; one day returning from Glen Urquhart with their father they sat down to rest near the Raven's Rock at Fasadh-an-Fitheach. A raven flew over and dropped a bone. Twelve of the sons handled it with curiosity, then, as the thirteenth put out his hand for it, his father prevented him, saying, 'If it augurs good fortune we have enough; if evil, we have too much.' Before the end of a year and a day the twelve who touched the bone were dead.

The remaining four, Iain Ruadh (Red John), Iain Caol (Slender John), Eobhan Ban (Fair Ewen), and Gilleasbuig (Archibald), were the founders of four of the five septs of the Macdonalds in the Glen. These four septs were by custom always buried feet to the east and on their backs, that they might have their faces towards Our Lord when at the Last Day He comes from the East. But the fifth sept, Slioched Alasdair Choire-Dho, though buried in the same old churchyard of Clachan Mercheird, were always buried feet to the west, that their first sight when waking at the Last Day may be their beloved Corri-Dho. The posture of burial must once have been held of great importance in the Celtic world. Egghan, King of Connaught, when dying of his wounds during war with the men of Ulster commanded that he should be buried upright, his red javelin in his hand and his face turned towards Ulster, as if still fighting his foes. As long as he so remained Connaught prevailed and Ulster lost. But the men of Ulster discovered the reason, dug him up and re-buried him facing the opposite way as if in retreat. It is recorded that Ulster was then victorious.

This old church of Merchard, of which the burial ground is all that remains, has a strange history. St. Erchard, more often called Merchard from Mo Erchard, My Erchard, a term of affection, was one of the very early Saints and went with two disciples to preach the Gospel in Strathglass. His attention was there drawn to a white cow which stood, day after day, gazing at a certain tree. She never 'bent her neck to the grass' yet always had plenty of milk and looked plump and well-liking. Puzzled, the saint decided to dig at the foot of the tree and there he found three bells, 'new and burnished as if fresh from their makers' hands'. He gave one each to his disciples and took one himself. It was then revealed to him that they must all three set out, each going his own way, and each must build a church where his bell rang for the third time. So they started. One went eastward and built the church of Glenconvinth, another westward and erected his church at Broadford in Skye; Merchard himself travelled southward in the direction of Glenmoriston. When he reached the hill called Suidh Merchard, Merchard's Seat, his bell rang its first ring and he rested there awhile, whence its name. It next rang at Ballintombuie and the saint stopped and drank from a spring there, since known as Fuaran Mhercheird, Merchard's Well; then he came down to the River Moriston and his bell rang for the third time, so there, near the river where the old graveyard still is, he built his church, Clachan Mhercheird. There he taught and preached and eventually died. He became the Glen's patron saint and has been known to intervene in its affairs repeatedly. Dr W. Mackay in his *Urquhart and Glenmoriston* tells how in olden times when a tenant died the proprietor had a right to his horse as a heriot. If the man left no horse, sheep or cattle to a horse's value could be taken instead. On one occasion, more than a thousand years after the Saint's death, a tenant died leaving no horse and his widow's sheep were taken by the law officer. That same night as the officer lay in bed, an unearthly voice spoke to him: 'I am great Merchard of the miracles, passing homeward in the night. Declare thou unto MacPhatrick (the proprietor) that the widow's sheep will never bring him any good.' The frightened officer hastened to the laird as early as he dared in the morning and the sheep were at once returned to the widow. Nor did the laird ever again demand a heriot.

The wonder bell remained in the church, curing all those sick or infirm who touched it in faith, until the old church began to crumble and fall into ruin. It was then moved out into the churchyard and placed upon a tombstone specially set aside for the purpose. From here it was stolen about 1870. This bell rang of itself when a funeral was approaching the church or a dead man was carried near it. On one occasion it was heard ringing urgently in the night. Alarmed, various men got together and went to see the cause. They found a dead man lying a few yards from the church, obviously murdered. A search was immediately begun for the murderer, who, thanks to the bell's timely warning, was quickly caught, his clothes still wet with his victim's blood.

At the further end of Glenmoriston comes Dun Dreggan, said to mean the dun of the great beast or dragon, and the Dun itself to take its name from the field (or place) of the Dragon nearby. There are various tales to account for the name. Very possibly the skeleton of some huge prehistoric animal really was found buried here. This Glen, as legend recounts, may well have once been such a swamp as these creatures are believed to have inhabited, and peat is a fine preservative. Others tell that a dragon (some say 'Grey Dog') dwelt here into human times and was ultimately slain by Fionn and his men after an epic battle and buried where it fell. Fionn then built a dun near his fallen foe to reassure the people of the valley who feared that dragon cubs might have survived their parent. In due course the dun naturally became a dwelling place of the Little People and the 'Wee Folk' of Glenmoriston were reputed very active. The particular clan or tribe who lived in Dundreggan were always very anxious to carry off the mothers of new-born babies to be wet nurses to their fairy children. They were more interested in doing this than in stealing the babies themselves. Ewen Macdonald of Dundreggan was out attending to his beasts on the night when his wife had her first-born son. A sudden gust of wind passed him and as it shook him he heard his wife's sigh in it. She sighed as she had sighed before her child was born and he, recognising the sound, flung his knife into the wind in the name of the Trinity, and his wife dropped safely to the ground beside him.

If a fairy child had a mortal foster-mother it gained a 'something' it could obtain no other way, so the Glenmoriston fairies believed. And more than once they successfully stole and kept a wife. As, in the words written by John M. Hay, one bereft husband sighed:

> The fairy folk have lured your face away
> Unto the land where one grows never old,
> Beyond the hollow hills and doors of day.

One night a man out late upon the hill heard the sound of singing —very sad and plaintive—coming out of the knoll of Dundreggan.

He bent to listen and heard a woman's voice chanting over and over again:

I am the wife of the Laird of Balnain
The Folk have stolen me over again.

He hurried to the house in question and there found that the owner was absent and his wife and baby son missing. Much worried, he sought out a priest who came back to the fairy knoll with him, blessed it and sprinkled it with holy water. Suddenly the night grew dark and there was a loud noise as of thunder; then the moon came out from behind a cloud and there was the woman, lying on the grass with her baby in her arms. She was exhausted as if she had travelled a long distance and could not tell how she got there.

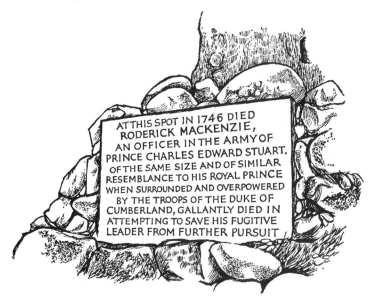

AT THIS SPOT IN 1746 DIED RODERICK MACKENZIE, AN OFFICER IN THE ARMY OF PRINCE CHARLES EDWARD STUART. OF THE SAME SIZE AND OF SIMILAR RESEMBLANCE TO HIS ROYAL PRINCE WHEN SURROUNDED AND OVERPOWERED BY THE TROOPS OF THE DUKE OF CUMBERLAND, GALLANTLY DIED IN ATTEMPTING TO SAVE HIS FUGITIVE LEADER FROM FURTHER PURSUIT

Some miles further, near Cean-na-Croc, the grave of one Roderick Mackenzie is to be seen. At least it is his grave in part, as one might say, his head being elsewhere. Why he has not become famous in song and story it is hard to see, for he undoubtedly gave his life that Prince Charles Edward might have the better chance of escape. He was a young officer of the Prince's army. After Culloden he, like others, escaped and went into hiding, in his case in Glenmoriston. Now Roderick excessively resembled the Prince in appearance. It is said that he heard a rumour that the Prince was in hiding in this district; no one knows how much he knew but what is known is that after lying safely hidden for some time he came out into the open and allowed the Government troops, who were searching the Glen, a good sight of his face. He was mistaken for Prince Charles Edward and the chase was on. In the end he was overtaken at Cean-na-Croc and turned at bay. He fought hard and bravely but at last fell dying of multiple wounds. As he died he cried clearly: 'Alas, you have slain your Prince.' The troops who had chased and killed him had no doubt at all but that he was Prince Charles Edward. One is even supposed to have expressed some anxiety as to the consequences of killing Royalty. They cut off Roderick Mackenzie's head, buried his body where it lay and carried the head in haste to Fort Augustus. There was no one there who knew the Prince well by sight so the head passed as his and was hastily pickled in a brine tub and sent south, and it was some time before the truth was discovered. Meanwhile pursuit of the Prince slackened; indeed in some districts it ceased altogether, and this gave him the chance to escape to France which he might otherwise have found impossible. A cairn marks the grave of Roderick Mackenzie. After he got safely away from Skye, Prince Charles Edward with three friends did make for Glenmoriston, there to be helped and sheltered and fed for three weeks by the 'Seven Men of Glenmoriston', themselves fugitives on his account. Two things are recorded of this time. When he left them the Prince gave each of them three guineas to remember him by—a curious gift to men who could have had £30,000 for his head by strolling down the Glen, but all he had to give. He also shook hands with each man. Two of them vowed never again to allow anyone, man, woman or child, to touch their right hands, and used their left hands for the rest of their lives.

The road through the Glen is very beautiful but also, despite many improvements, very curly. The big dam at Loch Cluanie is itself an interesting sight and its builders have been at much pains to avoid unduly injuring the beauties of the Glen. Through birch woods and oak woods and farm lands the road eventually comes out into some of the loneliest moorland in Scotland. In the days when Scotland had her own Kings this Forest of Cluanie was one of the King's royal forests, and deer still abound, or did a few years ago. But no one knows what numbers can survive the flooding of their old low-lying winter grazing under the hydro-electric scheme. It seems that starvation must drastically reduce the herds. A new road now runs along the hillside above the new loch. The making of this road and the remaking of the old one was an enormous task which occupied many years. Some unfortunates, among whom were my husband and I, had to traverse it frequently at that time and we ended up with an enormous respect for the firm, Watson's, which had the job in hand, and even more for their drivers. Never once were we held up by one of their lorries or machines if it could possibly be avoided, and though the constant traffic must have been infuriating, both to drivers and to road gangs, they were always pleasant and always ready to interrupt their work so as to make a way through for a passing car. It was the more noticeable because some other lorries, and even small cars, will at times hold up everyone behind them on this road for many miles. It is strange what bad driving manners some people have, even people who would be very shocked at the idea of doing an ill-mannered act in ordinary life.

At the western end of Loch Cluanie the road from Invergarry used to come in. The Tomdoun road leaves the main Inverness-Fort William one at Invergarry on the shores of Loch Oich. Passing the attractive Invergarry Hotel and little church, the latter at some times of year almost hidden in blossom, the road runs by the Garry river to Loch Garry itself. Lovely as Highland lochs usually are, Loch Garry has the added beauty in early summer of masses upon masses of rhododendrons, many growing wild in the woods. (Can anyone tell me what the riddle is to which half the answer is: 'And the other rode a dendron'?) The road holds firmly to the loch side till it reaches the pleasant fishing hotel of Tomdoun. The flat ground below the hotel was the scene of a battle between the Macmillans and the Grants. Some of the cairns erected over those killed in the battle may still be found.

At Tomdoun the road divides into two; one arm goes straight on past Loch Quoich to Loch Hourn. Loch Quoich must once have been the heart of a tale now forgotten. All that remains is the saying: 'The black tailor's short cut to Glen Quoich—round the world.' The second arm, the road to the right, has recently been closed to traffic. Instead, a new road now takes off from Loch Garry five miles before Tomdoun is reached and climbs rapidly over the high ground beside the Loch. It is a fine road with the most wonderful views of Loch Garry and, later, Loch Quoich and with many well-placed viewpoints. This road joins the Inverness-Glenshiel one about a mile east of the Cluanie Dam. It is a great time saver for all who come from or go to the West, but some of us regret the old road by Tomdoun which used to come out near Cluanie Inn, just west of the Loch, and was very beautiful. This old road, now closed, turns sharply to the right just beyond Tomdoun Hotel and begins to climb, up and up and up through pine woods and over bare moors to where, in hidden valleys far below, little bare peat lochs reflect the sky. It goes on over the pass which, in winter, is not infrequently blocked by snow or icy road surfaces, but once over it a fine panorama of the old royal Forest of Cluanie lies spread out below. My husband and I were driving from Cluanie to Glengarry one winter. Everything was frozen hard and a recent fall of snow had obliterated all wheel marks in the old snow on the road. The world was virgin white, without trace of life. In spite of our chains we wondered rather anxiously whether we would get over the high ground of the Pass; however, we did and were descending in a completely silent and uninhabited world when we saw a small frozen lochan in the heather to the right of the road and, on it, marks as of cart wheels, clear and unmistakeable in the new-fallen snow which covered the ice. Curious, we stopped and got out to see where they led. No sign or track of living thing was to be seen, we were miles from any house or cultivation and there was no trace of footmark, wheel mark or sledge mark in the snow on the loch shore, either where the wheel marks began on the snow-covered ice or where they ended, or indeed anywhere else. Much puzzled, we searched carefully. Nothing. On return to civilisation we tried to find out if anything could have been there. Nothing. Nothing had been or could have been there. And that was that.

Months later we were told that what we had seen must have been the marks of the Devil's coach wheels. He drives over the moors in winter and his coach wheel marks are often seen on lonely frozen lochs, but never a sign on land nor a sign of the horses that draw his coach. When these wheel marks are seen it is well to stay quiet indoors, for who knows what he seeks? And anyhow those who go prying may be found frozen, for he drives only when the weather is black hard and likely to remain so. But despite the risk his jet-black coach with its jet-black steeds has been seen driving at speed over the moors, both in Rannoch and over the Grampian slopes, leaving wheel tracks on many a small lonely ice-bound loch. It would be very interesting to know the true cause of this phenomenon, these wheel-like tracks, for they certainly do exist and appear to be not uncommon in mountain districts of the Highlands, and the tracks keep the right distance apart for cart or coach wheels. I have been told there are no hoof marks because the Devil's horses are spirits whereas his coach, used to carry mortals, must have earthly substance, but, if so, why do the wheels leave tracks only on ice? And whom does he carry off? And why?

The joint road continues past Cluanie Inn, over open moor and forestry land, to Glen Shiel. In the winter the deer come down from the hills to graze on the low ground between the River Shiel and the road. Hunger makes them so tame that on occasion we have had to get out of the car and drive a herd off the road before we could pass. They don't mind cars in the least. Indeed the smell of the exhaust gas is said to please them. A very sad tale is told of the deer in Glen Shiel. It happened in a deep cattle fold not far from Sgurr Urain. Once there was a girl who daily took her father's cattle out to graze in the Glen. There she met and loved a fairy—a little man who came out of one of the fairy knolls. The whole affair was, they believed, entirely secret and they wished it to remain so. But one day her brother went hunting and when he came home said to her (of course in Gaelic):

> I saw the dearest one yesterday
> Who was asking truly for thee.

at which she eagerly asked:

> How was my love when he remembered me?

only to get her brother's answer:

> I was smiting him sorely,
> To the North and to the South
> With my bright sword and my axe.
> With my left hand and my right.

Indignantly the girl rejoined:

> If thou hast slain the dear Oscar
> Arise and wash thy hands;
> May that be thy last washing
> After which thy body and bones will bleach.
> May there be never a month-old child in thy house.
> May there be no butter on thy milk
> May ...

But here her mother intervened and said:

> Mayst thou be split like the freshwater salmon
> Between thy two breasts and thy belly,
> May the poisonous serpent be beside thee
> Without thy ...

At this the girl was very frightened and she repented of her curse and said:

> The ill wish I made for my brother,
> Let it not be on him it rests at all,
> But on the rugged, brindled hills
> And on two thirds of the deer of the Glen.

Next day the rugged brindled hills were riven into fragments through the Glen and two thirds of the deer there were dead.

Glen Shiel is a queer glen, long, twisty, very narrow and steep, and so surrounded by mountains that the sun rarely penetrates it. It is wild and lonely and a little creepy, and in this cold, sunless glen there once lived a woman who spun for the fairies, and a good spinner she was and well the fairies paid her. But one day they fell out, for the Little People said she did not return all their lint, that she had not scraped the distaff tuft. No one had ever heard of such a scraping before and the woman was very angry and offended. However, though they no longer employed her the fairy women used to come to her to borrow her pot. When giving the pot to a fairy the woman would say:

> A pot deserves a bone
> And to be brought home whole;
> A smith deserves coal
> To heat cold iron.

and every day the pot would come home and something in it. But one day she forgot to say the spell on the pot and it did not come home. The woman was very angry for she had no other cooking pot. She went to the fairy mound to seek it and, seeing it, she seized it and, without speaking, carried it away. Then the fairy, gazing after her, said:

> Thou dumb woman there, thou dumb woman
> Who art come to us from the land of the cormorants,
> She seized the pot with her evil claw;
> Loose the noose and let slip the Fierce.

That was done and a great dog leapt after the woman and seized her by the leg. She screamed and was dead.

All this area is Fiann country and a giant suddenly appearing from among the rocks and clefts of the barren hills would not be surprising. It could easily have been they, not heavy rain, that started the landslide which cut the road here a few years ago, for instance. The scar it left on the hill side and some of the boulders it brought down are still to be seen. So too is the big stone in whose shelter Prince Charles Edward and his two guides are reputed to have slept peacefully through a raging storm.

Once my husband and I had to drive from Skye to Inverness on a wet and stormy winter night, arriving about midnight. From the outskirts of Kyle of Lochalsh to Dochfour (some 80 miles) we saw no living thing or sign of one; no car, no man, no sheep, no dog, no deer, no cow, not even a house showing a light (Cluanie Inn was closed), not even a hunting cat or the white tail of a rabbit. No sound but lashing rain in sheets and the wind howling in the hills. It was the eeriest and loneliest thing I have ever seen. *Anything* might have been about. We did not even see the spectre warriors fighting a ghostly battle in the Glen itself, though this is said to be not infrequently visible. There was once a Battle of Glen Shiel. It was fought as late as 1719, between the King's troops under General Wrightman and a force of Spaniards who had landed in the West to help the 'Old Chevalier'. Probably this was the last foreign invasion of Britain and the King's troops were completely victorious. Nothing more was ever heard of the Spanish invaders but it is said that on nights of low cloud when the mist whirls and twists around the mountains they can be seen busy as they were in life, not only fighting the King's men but marching wearily up the Pass. The men of both armies are there too, burying their dead.

Glen Shiel ends in some lovely country with the hills reflected in a reed-covered loch near Shiel Bridge. Here the road divides; that to the left crosses Mamratagan to Glenelg and that to the right runs along Loch Duich to Kyle of Lochalsh. Both roads end with a ferry to Skye.

Highland Pistol

SHIEL BRIDGE
TO KYLE OF LOCHALSH

Farewell to MacKenneth, Great Earl of the North,
The Lord of Lochcarron, Glenshiel and Seaforth;

★ ★ ★ ★ ★

For a far foreign land he has hoisted his sail,
Farewell to Mackenzie, High Chief of Kintail.
O, swift be the galley and hardy her crew,
May her captain be skilful, her mariners true,

★ ★ ★ ★ ★

May he hoist all his canvas from streamer to deck
But, O, crowd it higher when wafting him back,
Till the cliffs of Skooroora and Conan's glad vale
Shall welcome Mackenzie, High Chief of Kintail.

MURDOCH MATHESON; translated by
Sir W. Scott

AFTER SHIEL BRIDGE the road runs through the old
Mackenzie country of Kintail. In later centuries their chief
lived at Brahan Castle near Strathpeffer but in the early
days of the clan Kintail was their homeland. An old riddle asked:
'What are the three curses of a farmer?' to which the answer was:
'May frost, July mist and the Tutor of Kintail.' A 'Tutor' in the
Highlands of olden times meant the regent for an infant Chief,
and in his hands lay the welfare of his Clan. The Tutor of Kintail
did much for the clan but it is said to have been he who condemned
the Castle of Eilean Donnan as too primitive and Kintail as too
remote to be the seat of a Chief. He built Brahan Castle for his
ward and moved the Clan's centre away from Kintail and the
West—hence a certain unpopularity.

Round the head of Loch Duich goes the road and past the
little church of Kintail on its hillock overlooking the water. A
man once committed suicide in Loch Duich and was buried in

this little churchyard, to the north of the church, buried with his head, not his feet, to the east as is becoming for a suicide. But as a result of his act the herring left Loch Duich. The fishers waited for two years but the fish did not return. (Seven years is the usual length of the herring's absence after a murder or a suicide in their water.) Then the fishermen grew tired of waiting and one dark night they dug up the suicide's body from the churchyard and carried it to the top of a high hill where Inverness-shire and Ross-shire meet; here they buried it again, hoping to appease the herring. The herring were duly appeased and returned to the loch. A similar burial and for the same reason is said to have taken place on the summit of Aird Dhubh.

Loch Duich herring seem easily perturbed, for they are said to have been absent from duty when, disabled by storm, a 'foreign vessel' came into the Loch. By the custom of the time MacRae of Inverinate might have treated both the vessel and its cargo as his by right, but instead he helped the crew to make and fit a new mast from his woods and allowed them to depart in peace. Before leaving, the captain, to show his gratitude, presented MacRae with a small silver herring. This highly magic little fish had only to be laid in the waters of the loch to attract herring in shoals from far and near. It proved, as may be imagined, a most valuable possession.

The road runs through the Inverinate woods, then up and up, past mountain burns and through fields of the wild iris, to a high summit looking down on the sea-lochs below. There are few views to equal this one in Scotland. To the south-east the Five Sisters of Kintail lift their blue heads above their scarves of mist, to the west lies Eilean Donnan Castle on its rock (perhaps the most photographed spot in the Highlands) guarding the blue Kyles; and in the distance stand the hills of Skye.

Loch Duich is a loch of many stories. Once there lived in Kintail an old man who had seven beautiful daughters. He was much worried, for he felt that they were so beautiful that they should marry well but his farm was in a lonely glen on the shore of Loch Duich and he really did not see how or whom they were to marry at all. Every day they grew more beautiful and desirable and every day the old man worried more. One night, however, there was a great storm and into the Loch for shelter came a fine ship. Once she had been very fair indeed but now she was battered by the waves and with her sails in shreds. Her owners, two young brothers, thankfully accepted the old man's offer of help and of timber to refit her. The youths were very handsome, with red-gold hair and with eyes blue-grey like the sea; they were tall, too, and stronger than any in the glen. Needless to say, the seven sisters saw and loved them. Needless also to say, the brothers were enchanted by the beauty of their young hostesses. For many months work on the ship continued. Everything a ship could need was done. She was careened on the shore and scraped, fresh sails were sewn by the sisters and fitted, and so forth. But at last the day came when they could find no further excuse to linger in the Loch and the two brothers took their courage in their hands and, coming to the old farmer, asked for his two youngest daughters in marriage. The old man went to consult the seven. The two youngest were delighted; they were very willing to sail happily away with their lovers, they declared. But the five elder sisters wept and at last the eldest daughter said to their father: 'We do not think it right that our youngest sisters should be married before us; let the suitors choose according to age as is proper.' The old man brought back this answer to the young sea-captains. The younger looked very dismayed but the elder replied: 'What your daughters say is right and wise and we do not deny it but we, my brother and I, are ourselves younger brothers, having five brothers older, handsomer and richer than ourselves. When they see our wives they will most certainly desire to wed your elder daughters. It would not, therefore, be proper for us to ask the hands of the two eldest sisters.' And so it was agreed, the two young men married the two youngest sisters and sailed away with them to Ireland, first making firm and solemn promise that their five brothers would come soon out of Ireland to woo and win their brides.

Winter passed and summer passed and winter came again but no ship sailed in from Ireland with five eager bridegrooms on board. Meanwhile the fame of the girls' beauty spread throughout Kintail and many a young man found business which led him to the farm, there to offer for the hand of one of the remaining five daughters. But the girls would have none of them.

'His hair is not like spun gold but mere mouse-colour,' said one.

'I will marry no man under whose arm I cannot walk,' said another when a small but rich young farmer proposed for her hand.

And so it went on while their father grew older and more worried. One day he went out, killed a stag and carried it to the Grey Magician of Coire Dhuinid who was famed for his wisdom. The Wise Man listened and promised to come and talk to the sisters. He came and told them of how he had gazed into the black pool of the corrie and had learned there that no such young men as their brother-in-law had described existed. They were waiting only for shadows, he said. Let them therefore be wise in time and marry while they could, for that way happiness and safety lay. But the sisters would not.

'Are we to be farmers' wives while our sisters are queens in Ireland?' asked the eldest.

'Are we to live and die in Kintail,' cried the second, 'while our sisters sail out into the world?'

'Are we to be poor, and our sisters rich?' asked the third angrily.

'I have seen him in dreams and I love him,' sobbed the fourth, 'I will marry no man but him.'

'I have seen my lover's face in the loch water,' said the youngest firmly, 'and I will be faithful to him until death.'

So the magician left and the years passed and the old farmer grew aged and feeble and *very* worried. He sent again to the Grey Magician, who came and for long they sat over the peat fire talking; then the magician left. Next day the old man died and the five daughters found themselves alone in the world. But with night came the magician.

'Yesterday,' he said, 'I talked with your father and promised him to hold you in my protection. It is time you married.'

'No,' said five voices.

'Do you wish to wait for ever for your dream bridegrooms?' asked the wizard. 'Think well before you answer,' he added, 'for in your answers lies your fate.'

'We will wait and watch forever,' they replied.

'In that case,' said the magician in practical tones, 'I will turn you into five mountains and place you at the head of Loch Duich so that you can wait and watch forever as you desire, safe from the evils and dangers of the world.'

So the sisters became five hills, the beauty that was theirs in life remains theirs still and as 'The Five Sisters of Kintail' they wait and watch for the sails of the ship which never comes, the ship they even yet believe will still come and bring their lovers.

It is to Loch Duich, too, that seal-people come of an evening and it has been known even to tempt mermen into the shallows. The seals are a gentle, kindly folk but very unhappy. You have only to look at their eyes to see that. They do not fear humans half as much as most wild creatures do, and if you go down to the shore and there locate a seal swimming along with its bullet head above water like a dog, and you stand on the shore and bark to it it will, after the first moment of surprise, answer you. Then a lengthy if limited conversation can be carried on as it will remain near as long as you will bark. It is an unkind thing to do though, for it encourages that particular seal to look on humans as pleasant, barking creatures and makes it more vulnerable in consequence to the seal-hunters who want its liver to make seal oil. Seal oil in the highlands was, and in some places still is, what cod liver oil is to the South. If properly made—the oil-yielding parts must be melted down over a slow fire but never allowed to boil for if it reaches the boiling point the good will be lost—it is extremely effective for the colds and coughs of winter or for the child that does not thrive. But few nowadays have the patience to make it properly. The Health Service will provide, so why bother?

It has long been believed that seals were human beings under enchantment and that they are allowed to resume their human forms for short periods, 'to keep them unhappy' think some. When the time for the seals to assume human shape arrives they come ashore, slough their seal skins and hide them carefully beneath a rock or in a convenient cave. There are many stories of men finding and hiding a skin. If this happens, the seal concerned is unable to rejoin the others when their human time is up but must remain on shore, utterly helpless, the slave of the hider of the skin. Usually it is a beautiful maiden whose fur is so concealed, and the seal maidens are very beautiful indeed, with dark hair and large brown eyes. The story is told of three brothers who went down one evening to fish off the rocks in Loch Duich not far from the castle. It was a wonderful moonlight night, no good for the fishing, and as they were looking idly about them they saw a number of seals' heads bobbing along towards the shore. They hid and watched the seals land, slip off their skins, roll them neatly into bundles and hide them beneath the large stones with which the beach was covered. Each seal chose its own stone. Then the seal folk began to run and leap upon the beach or lie stretching in the moonlight, rejoicing in their freedom. Among them were three particularly beautiful girls and the three young men loved them on sight. Animated by a single thought, they crept nearer and nearer to the stones where the skins had been left, carefully hiding behind boulders as they went. At length they were within reach of the skins; each seized the skin of a maiden and fled away with it. They concealed the skins carefully, then returned to the beach to wait. As the grey of dawn began to lighten the sky a curlew called and at this signal each seal made for his or her skin, but the three maidens had no skins. The maidens wrung their hands and wept as the first rays of the rising sun struck the beach and the seals, all weeping also, slid back into the sea leaving the three frightened girls clinging together at the water's edge,.for well they guessed the fate of their skins. The boys, once the seal host had departed, came down on to the shore and spoke to the maidens, explaining how much they admired them and that they wished to marry them. The maidens only wept and begged them to return their skins. The two elder brothers began to tell the girls how much they loved them and what a good life they would have once they were married. A dress of silk, a bed of softest feathers, they promised, butter, too, and cream. But the maidens wept on and trembled as an aspen trembles when no wind stirs it; and the youngest brother said nothing. 'What will you give your bride?' demanded his brothers, 'speak, man, offer her something.' But the youngest brother said nothing, for his heart was stirred with a great love and he knew the gift that he must offer.

At length daylight came and the three brothers took each his seal maiden and returned each to his own house and the doors were closed. The youngest brother alone came out again and went to his peat stack. When he returned he bore his bride gift —a seal skin—in his arms. When he opened the door there was his seal maiden crouched by the large box bed, still trembling with great eyes of fear. The boy did not speak, he could not, but he held out to her her seal skin and she grabbed it (there is no other word) and with fingers clumsy with haste she dressed herself in it. Then the young man opened the house door and away she went, slip, slither, down over the grass, into the sea and away. The boy went to milk the cows. When his brothers, each with a good, submissive wife, learned what he had done they started to tease him. But he turned on them so fiercely that they, astonished and afraid, did not mention seals to him again. But on the ninth night they fastened house and door and barn with care. The youngest brother did not trouble. He went down to the sea shore and sat on a stone openly to watch the seals come in, for he felt he could no longer spy on her. The seals came in in hordes, more than he had ever seen before, took human form and hurried off in every direction, searching, searching. His maiden came too and looked shyly at him, then she too began to search, but half-heartedly, until an old man with a fine face spoke to her and together they came to the boy.

'It is my duty to thank you, Sir,' said the man with curious old-world courtesy, 'for liberating my daughter, though not for the fright you gave her.' He spoke coldly. Then he looked up and caught the boy's gaze fixed upon the maiden. His expression changed and he added in warmer tones: 'Should you need us we are your servants. Fionagalla, do your duty.'

The seal maid ran lightly up to the door of the young man's house, opened it and vanished within. The boy rose, bowed to her father (a rather clumsy imitation of the old man's own bow) and followed her. He found bannocks baking and the maiden busy setting the house to rights. He tried to help. Soon she was smiling at his efforts. When the dawn-grey lightened the sky he accompanied her back to the beach. And so it became the custom for the boy to make a tally of a hazel twig and mark off each day till the ninth and for the sea-maiden to make a tally of a razor-shell and mark it also, and every ninth night they spent together in the little house in a happiness nine times greater than was ever in the world before.

Meanwhile the elder brothers grew fat and lazy, their docile wives doing all the work. One day the eldest brother's children were at play in the barn when they explored an old tub and in the bottom lay a brown fur seal skin. They ran in to their mother with their find. One look and the seal woman seized it from them, dressed quickly in it and, with a parting wave to her children, dived back into the sea and was never seen again. The second brother was much concerned, specially when his children asked him what it was that their mother searched for all day while he was out. He thought and thought and at last decided that the only way to hide the skin completely and for ever was to burn it. So he made a fire of straw and laid the skin upon it. There was an instant explosion and the man was thrown to the ground; burning sparks had fired the thatched roof of his house he saw when he rose and hurried over, calling to his wife to bring water. No reply. His wife lay dead within. She had died from burns.

In the long ago days a young girl lived with her father and stepmother on the shore of Loch Duich. They owned a tiny house there. She had the misfortune to have a very evil stepmother and though her father loved her dearly he was no match for his wife who one day in his absence turned the child, for she was little more, out of the house, forbidding her ever to return on pain of cursing. The child went down to the seashore and there, weary and frightened and cold, she sat and wept. A merman saw and pitied her; he raised himself from the sea and tried to comfort her and the girl sobbed out her story. 'Come with me to my palace below the sea,' he begged. 'I will care for you.' But she would not, certain that her father would come in search of her. But the night grew wild and cold and her father did not come, for his wife had told him that his daughter had been drowned and the body carried out by the tide. But as the tide rose the girl, exhausted with weeping, decided to wait for it and go where it took her. It was the merman, not the tide, that came for her, however, and he carried her down to his undersea palace.

There she learned that he was a king and rich beyond anything she could imagine. They were married and lived in quiet happiness but in the spring of the year the girl always grew homesick and her husband would rise to the surface and return with news of her father, gathered from the wild duck, the geese and the rock pigeons who were his messengers. One day he told her that her stepmother was dead but that before her death she had ruined her husband who had now neither cow nor sheep, neither a horse to plough with nor seed to sow.

The little earth queen begged eagerly: 'Oh, might I not send him one of my pearls or a golden cup? We have so much and he has nothing.' 'Neither our pearls nor our gold cups would be useful,' he told her, 'but wait.' He summoned a porpoise and spoke to him in a tongue the earth girl had never learnt. 'I have sent to a wreck for earth money,' said the king. Soon the porpoise returned with a bag of gold coins in his mouth, heavier than she could lift, but her husband wrapped it in his tail, took her in his arms and bore her safely back to the shore by her father's house. Leaving the gold hidden under a rock she ran home and great indeed was the happiness in the little farm that night. Her father took some of the gold next day and set out for Dingwall where he bought both grain and beasts. His daughter went down to the shore in search of her husband. He was waiting for her. She asked leave to stay until her father found a wife and the merman agreed, telling her to meet him there each evening. In due course a good wife was found and then, on the ninth day of the ninth month, the little earth wife went down to the sea shore. This time she did not speak, there was no need, for, her task completed, she slid quietly into the grey sea waves by his side and he carried her home, never to be seen on earth again.

From the summit the road runs down an equally steep hill to the village of Dornie at its foot. Here is Dornie Bridge, across the entrance to Loch Long, a great boon to the Isles when opened in 1942, and here, close by the bridge, stands the Castle of Eilean Donnan, a castle with a somewhat chequered history. The first castle on the island, which is believed to have been called after St. Donnan the Martyr of Eigg, was built by Alexander II on, says tradition, the site of a much older fort or dun. It was intended

Eilean Donnan Castle

as a defence against the Danes and Norsemen and the King made
one Kenneth Matheson his first Constable of Eilean Donnan.
Kenneth's descendants were known as MacKennich, Sons of
Kenneth, which soon became Mackenzie. After some centuries,
during which the castle had been both destroyed and rebuilt, the
Tutor of Kintail, as has been said, made Brahan Castle the new
seat of the Clan and the MacRaes became Constables of the
Castle for the Mackenzies of Seaforth as they now were.

It would appear that at the time of the Rising of 1715 the castle was being held for the King. A farmer nearby thought this was a mistake and offered to place it in the hands of the local Jacobites. This he did quite simply. On a hot morning he called on the Garrison Commander and told him that he expected the weather to break in a few hours, his corn was still out and unless the Governor would lend him the men to get it in it would be ruined. Food, as both knew, was scarce and owing to the Troubles would soon be scarcer. All seemed quiet in the district and the Governor of the castle led out all his men to help get in the harvest. In his absence the Jacobites seized the fortress. That night there was great rejoicing in the castle and men were seen dancing reels on its tower in the moonlight. A few hours later came news of defeat. Later again the castle was partly demolished by gunfire from H.M.S. *Worcester* in 1719. After being a ruin for about 200 years it has been rebuilt by Colonel John McRae-Gilstrap to be as nearly as possible as it was, much of the old walls fortunately remaining.

There are many stories of the Castle. One is rather curious. It claims that for long there was enmity between the Macdonnels of Glengarry and the Mackenzies and that the constant fear of raids was undermining the morale of both clans. At length the Wise Raven of Glengarry, having enticed Macdonnell's heir into the hills, spoke to him very seriously on the subject. Acting on the Raven's advice, young Glengarry got a contingent of fighting men from his father and successfully attacked and captured Eilean Donnan Castle and the heir to the Chief of Clan Mackenzie with it. Now in a strong position, he was able to dictate terms. These were laid down by the Wise Raven and led to a lasting peace between the clans.

Serpents (adders) were very common in this part of the Highlands. They were believed to sleep through the winter and appear on Bride's Day (February 1st), and this should be their greeting:

> Early on the Feast of Bride
> The daughter of Ivor will come from her hole
> I will not harm the daughter of Ivor
> And the daughter of Ivor will not harm me.

Some of the charms addressed to the serpent hail her as 'noble

Queen', which is comprehensible, but no one seems to know why 'daughter of Ivor'. Legend in this district, however, says that in the very early days of Eilean Donnan a Constable of the Castle married a Russian wife who was a very powerful witch and her father, whose name was Ivor, was an even more potent wizard. The snakes were her familiars and on occasion she herself would take snake form. That is why there were so many snakes in this district. No one dared to harm them in case they should accidentally kill the daughter of Ivor and her father or husband would avenge her. On the other hand it is said that Mrs Macleod of Stein (Flora Macdonald's eldest daughter) filled a stocking with peat every St. Bride's Day and stamped it flat as a symbol of bruising the serpent's head.

The road continues by the side of Loch Alsh as far as Ardelve. Near here is a cave in the cliffs, said to be an old 'Pict's House' for it is lined and roofed with slabs of stone and although the entrance is narrow and unimportant-looking the cave itself is of considerable size.

After Ardelve come Balmacarra, now a National Trust property, and Balmacarra House, now a school, and then the road turns slightly inland over the base of a peninsula to Kyle of Lochalsh.* The road soon passes a lovely small loch with tiny islands. Tradition, but a very shaky tradition, claims this as the site of a battle between, perhaps, Mathesons, whose country this was, and a Sutherland raiding party. Both chiefs were killed and were buried together in harmony on this tiny island.

The road, through very beautiful country and views, runs down to Kyle of Lochalsh—a village of roses where the sun, one feels, always shines. From here the main car ferry to Skye functions. Not quite fifty years ago this ferry was a rowing boat with two planks across it. The car drove on to the planks (if it could) and was then lashed on. If seas rose while crossing, the lashings would be cast off, leaving the car free and ready to slide over the side if the boat began to roll, thus leaving the boat safe. Changed days!

* During the post-war housing shortage, a cave close to the roadside just after Balmacarra was occupied by a family who lived there for some years for want of better accommodation.

It has long been held in the Highlands that she who borrows or steals a burning peat from her neighbour's fire can then, should she wish, drain the milk from her neighbour's cow or the cream from her milk and have it herself. Indeed she can, if she wishes, take the substance out of all that the unfortunate neighbour possesses. Apparently such a belief is not only widespread but also old. Once there were two giants; they were brothers, Akin and Rhea, living near one another in two strong castles on the slopes above the Kyles, and were such great friends that they were almost inseparable. Being giants, they had no difficulty in leaping over to Skye when need arose. One day the younger brother, Rhea, returning from a deer hunt in the Island, found his fire out and his castle cold and comfortless. He passed on to Akin's castle where the fire had been well smoored and he soon blew it into flames and warmed himself at it. Then he prepared to go home, taking with him a smouldering peat ember to re-start his own fire. Unfortunately at that moment Akin returned and, finding his brother taking fire and with it, if he so willed, the substance of all he possessed, was furious, for he was a somewhat hasty-tempered young giant, and he began to fling rocks and boulders after him. The size and number that he threw can be judged by those still to be seen peppering the low ground today and testifying both to his strength and excessively wild aim and to the heinousness of the offence. But unfortunately his aim really *was* wild. He meant to frighten his brother, show his displeasure and teach him a lesson. But, alas!, one of the larger boulders caught Rhea between the shoulders; he tripped, fell, and, half stunned, rolled into the sea and was drowned. Kylerhea has ever since borne his name. Akin was desperately unhappy without him. Rhea was equally unhappy without Akin. One evening Akin returned cold and miserable from hunting, no longer for pleasure but only for food. He found the fire in his castle a cheerful blaze and, kneeling by it and blowing up the flames, the spirit of Rhea. Realising that he was forgiven and that Rhea had come for him, he immediately drowned himself in the Kyle which now bears his name, and the two spirits departed together in perfect happiness for the Blessed Isles.

SHIEL BRIDGE TO GLENELG

The door of Fionn is always open and the name of his hall
is the stranger's home. None ever went sad from Fionn
(Old saying)

THE ROAD over Mamratagan to the Glenelg-Kylerhea
ferry was a very popular one before the opening of Dornie
Bridge in 1942 as it enabled cars to reach Skye without
crossing a second ferry. Also, Mamratagan is no mean hill, even
for the West Coast, and from the road over it there is a series of
wonderful views, although the hillside is now forested and as the
trees grow taller views will grow fewer. 'Mam' is very common
in the names of swelling, rounded hills in the West Highlands
but was also used in the Isles to describe a swelling of the body
of any kind, including mumps. So, by a natural association of
ideas, in the olden days the local 'wise' man or woman would
banish such an ill to the nearest hill of the same name.

Mamratagan was one of the favourite hills for this practice
and must be positively alive with mumps germs and other bac-
teria in banishment there. The procedure was complicated. First
a suitable hill must be chosen and it must be known to the patient;
then the swellings must be divided into three imaginary sections,
a basin of pure water must be at hand and a needle and an axe be
dipped in it. The needle is then placed against one of the three
parts of the swelling and the axe brought down as if to fall upon
it and drive it in with great force, but at the last moment the axe
is diverted to a piece of wood. This is done to each of the three
parts in turn. While striking, the 'wise one' recites an appropriate
charm. In the case of Mamratagan it was:

> Be this stroke upon the Mam of Domhaillean,
> Be this stroke upon the Mam of Gleann Eilg,
> Be this stroke upon the Mam of Ratagan,
> In the name of the Father and the Son and the Holy Spirit.

All present must reply: 'Amen. Thy pang be in the ground, thy pain be in the earth.' Within three days the patient should recover. I never heard tell of a mountain that was any the worse.

The connection here between the disease and the cure is easy to see but some of the most attractive of the charms from this part of the world seem to have very little connection at all with the cure desired. For instance, to cure toothache one must repeat the Charm Against Toothache, as follows:

> The charm placed by Columba
> About the right knee of Maol Iodha
> Against pain, against sting, against poison,
> Against tooth disease, against bodily disease.
>
> Said Peter unto James
> 'I get no rest from the toothache,
> It is with me lying down and rising up
> And leaping on my two soles.'
>
> Said Christ, answering the problem,
> 'The toothache and the rune
> Shall not henceforth abide in the same head.'*
> (Of course, in Gaelic the verses rhyme)

Kylerhea in Skye and Glenelg on the mainland were much beloved of the Feinn and they were believed to have lived in Glenelg. At a place called (according to A. R. Forbes in his *Place Names of Skye*) Imir nam Fear Mora, Field of the Big Men, in Glenelg, there were some large burial mounds, traditionally the graves of the Feinn. Macpherson's *Ossian* and the controversy to which it gave rise resulted in a revival of interest in such matters and one day in the early nineteenth century two of these grave mounds were opened in the presence of 'a number of local gentlemen of repute' including a parish minister. In them are said to have been found stone coffins enclosing skeletons of two men and a woman, all considerably larger than life size as it is known today. It is believed that a doctor examined the two best preserved skeletons and estimated their heights when alive as having been, one approximately 8½ feet and the other almost 11 feet and said that they appeared strong-boned and well proportioned.

---

* These Translations from *Carmina Gadelica*.

These are not by any means the only 'Fiann graves' known in the North. Fionn himself was, in tradition, buried near Killin in Perthshire, although some have claimed the honour for a mound near the shore of little Loch Killin in Inverness-shire. Grainne, Fionn's wife, lies beneath a cairn on the summit of Ben na Cailleach in Skye, just across the water from Glenelg. Ossian

An ancient Dun, Glenelg

had many different endings, going direct to Heaven or to the Isle of the Blest, or living still, asleep beneath a mountain. But Perthshire says that he was buried just like any other man of his rank and time, in a stone coffin in the Sma' Glen, and that here his bones would be resting still but for General Wade. At this point we come into history. When Wade's men were preparing the foundations of his road to the North, they came upon an old stone cist or coffin of great age. This was opened and seen to contain a very large skeleton. But the men of the Highland clans who were working on the road became much upset when they saw what had been done, and explained that these were the bones of the great Ossian and should not have been disturbed nor his grave opened. The consequences might be appalling. Indeed, so angry and frightened were they that the young engineer in charge of that section thought it unwise to proceed without new and exact orders, and so sent a message to General Wade. He replied that all work on that sector was to cease until he himself arrived; he would ride over next day. In the night the bones and the heavy stone coffin which had held them disappeared and next day the workmen denied all knowledge of them. It appeared that none of them had ever seen a coffin or bones, nor heard of Ossian. In fact, no one knew anything about anything. But some soldiers in camp nearby had had sentries out and one of these had reported large numbers of men on the move. The sentry claimed to have seen a long procession of torches moving through the gloom of the night mist and to have heard wild, unearthly chanting sweeping by on the wind. Where Ossian's bones, if his they were, now lie, no one knows. But it does appear from these large skeletons and from the old songs and stories that there must once have been in the Highlands a tribe or clan of men larger and perhaps more civilised than their neighbours. That there are such large races has just been demonstrated by the discovery of a tribe in Africa considerably above normal height, and the Maharajah of Mysore always had giants as his State doorkeepers, men about 8 feet tall, at least as lately as 1943.

Traditionally the Feinn were fair and very tall, not quite 'giants' in the fairy tale sense but larger than men, say 9 to 10 feet in height; 'his fault is the fault of Fionn' was said in Gaelic of a little man, because Fionn's only fault is believed to have been his small size. He was smaller than his men, only 8 feet high or so some claim. But others say 'as long in the head as Fionn was in the leg'. The Feinn were strong and swift of foot, great fighters and hunters, and above all brave, courteous and just. They came to Scotland from Ireland. Their Chief was Fionn and under him were several families or clans, each with its own title to fame. Their six great assets were said to be: The Luck (or Wisdom) of Fionn, the Hand of Gaul, Oscar's rapid blows, Ossian's quickness at play, Caoilte's hard running, and Comal's planning of the battle. It was said, too, that 'their banner never went back though the grey earth trembled'. Like other heroes, they had their butt; this was 'the Mischief of the Feinn, quick-tempered, rash and meddlesome Conon, who was always in trouble. He once spied upon the wives of the Feinn as they went about their own concerns on the slopes of Mamratagan. The women, determined on revenge, laid a trap for him, into which he walked and lost all his hair. Poor bald Conon was much teased, so, sore and angry, he decided to leave Glenelg for a time and visit those of his friends who had died and whom he believed he would find in Ifrinn (Hell). They, he felt sure, would be glad to see him and would know nothing of the jokes being made at his expense. But he forgot the fiends who guard and rule Ifrinn and soon found himself engaged in single combat with their Chief. Walter Scott describes the fight as: ' "Claw to claw," as Conon said to Satan, "and the Devil take the shortest nails." '

The Feinn came to protect Scotland, and the little men there, from the raiders from Lochlann and they possessed certain magic gifts, chief of which was Fionn's Tooth of Wisdom which, if he pressed it, both could and would tell him all he needed to know. Stories of the Feinn are as widespread throughout the Highlands as are stories of King Arthur and his knights in England, but Argyll and Inverness-shire, including Skye, seem to have been their main haunts. Mamratagan, as has been already said, was very much their country. Here they hunted the deer and the wild boar, here the Yellow Magician turned Grainne, Fionn's wife, into a white hind. Here, too, it is said that Bran the great hound found Fionn's son Ossian and protected him from the hound pack who mistook him for a deer like his mother.

There are very many versions of the story of Grainne's enchantment and the birth of her son Ossian or his finding by his father Fionn. Campbell of Islay, the gatherer of a famous collection of old Highland stories, is reputed to have known fourteen. Indeed the tale of the white hind may well have as many forms as the rhyme about the Missionary who ate (or was eaten by) the Cassowary. In it, only three things were constant—a missionary, a cassowary and Timbuctoo. So all versions of the White Hind tale contain Fionn, his wife Grainne (who is changed to a white hind) and their son Ossian. Here is one which I have heard of Mamratagan.

At one time the Feinn lived in Glenelg and hunted on Mamratagan and it was here that Grainne's old nurse came to Fionn to beg his aid for her nursling. From here too Fionn set out to save Grainne from the clutches of a many-headed giant. Before this he had had, as was the fashion of the time, a fairy-love from a dun nearby. This fairy maid was lovely and charming but, like all the fairy people, she could not grow old. 'Grow old along with me, The best is yet to be' could never be applied to a fairy love affair. And as Fionn matured from youth to manhood he slowly and unconsciously outgrew his fairy love. Her youthful naiveté and sweetness began to irritate him and as his own wider understanding developed his need of a more responsible helpmeet grew greater. When he was thrown into the company of Grainne on their long and dangerous journey back from the giant's castle and she risked her life to save his, he found in her all he sought in a wife, and they were married. Usually, fairy loves accepted the position but Fionn's did not and on the day when Grainne's baby son was born she waited nearby and, in the temporary absence of Grainne's women, laid a spell upon her that she should become a white hind. And so she did. But, not realising what had happened, Grainne licked her baby's face, deer fashion, and on his forehead sprouted a patch of deer's hair. Horrified, she fled. When Fionn returned from hunting and found her missing, he pressed his Tooth of Wisdom which showed him what had happened.

Against the power of the spell which his discarded fairy love had bought at great cost from the Yellow Magician he was powerless. Nevertheless, he constantly sought for the white hind but never found her until she lay dying. Meanwhile her little son Ossian grew up with the Feinn and above all things loved to accompany them on their hunting trips. On one of these occasions he became separated from his companions and, just as he realised that he was lost, he saw a very beautiful white hind. What a prize to bring back to his teachers! Knowing nothing of his mother's story, he flung his spear at the hind but most fortunately, being both young and excited, missed her. To his surprise the hind did not gallop off but stood looking at him with lovely sad eyes and said: 'Don't harm me, Ossian, I am thy mother under the Fith-Fath (enchantment). Thou art weary, hungry and thirsty; come home with me, fawn of my heart.' Ossian went with her and she led him to a solid-seeming rock face on the mountain side where she pressed the stone, a door slid open and they entered. As soon as the door closed behind them she resumed human form and Ossian saw before him the loveliest woman he could imagine. The house was brightly lit, though not by sun or moon or stars, and well furnished. Grainne told him her story as she prepared food and drink for him. Then, while soft music played, he ate 'his seven full satisfactions'. At last he said he must rejoin the Feinn hunting on the hills near by. His mother gave him three kisses and let him go. When he looked back no sign of the rock door could he see, or ever again find.

Ossian thought he had spent three days with his mother but on earth it was three years. It was then and for her that Ossian made his first song—a song to warn her against the men and the hounds of the Feinn.

> If thou be my mother and thou a deer,
> Arise ere the sun rises on thee.
> Travel the hills ere the heat of the hunt,
> Beware thou the men of the Feinn
> Beware thou the hounds of the Feinn,
> Avoid the bitch of the black tail,
> Avoid Bran, son of Buidheag, foe of deer.
> (and so on for many verses)

Then he left the rock wall, outside which he had sung, and went to tell Fionn. And it is said that the Feinn never again hunted on that hillside so long as the white hind lived. But Fionn, with Bran on leash, searched it inch by inch and day by day, but Grainne he never saw for the evil of his fairy love sent her to other pastures.

Ossian is perhaps the most famous of all the Feinn, better remembered than even Fionn himself, for he was their bard and poet, and so lived on. One story tells how he outlived his beloved only son Oscar, and Fionn himself, and then agreed to go to the Islands of the Blest with the beautiful Niam, daughter of the King of the Land of the Living.

Redder was her cheek than the rose,
Fairer her face than swan upon the wave,
More sweet the taste of her balsam lips
Than honey mingled with red wine.

She carried Ossian on her horse across the western sea waves to where, she promised him, 'Fleeting time shall not bend thee nor death nor decay shalt thou see,' and the Feinn raised three shouts of mourning as he went. But after some 300 years of living the life of a lotus eater in the Islands of perpetual spring and perpetual sunshine, where all flowers always bloomed, where trees bore fruit and flower on one branch, where birds ever sang, he grew homesick for the Highlands, his old haunts and friends and, above all, for mist and rain. Niam, knowing all was changed, bade an eagle carry him low over the land, wherever he would. He returned to Tir-nan-Og horrified by what he had seen. Men, he said, had become small and wizened and weak; women were no longer lovely but pitiful, and they had lost all the knowledge of older times. He begged Niam to let him return to earth and teach them. This, she told him, was not possible. Should he touch the earth he would grow old and blind and wizened and vanish in dust. At last, however, she agreed to give him a horse which would carry him over the sea to Scotland and, so long as he did not dismount nor touch earth, he would be safe. Ossian promised only to teach men how to build houses, kindle fire, cook food and so on, and not himself to dismount even for a moment. He rode across the sea to a beach and soon had a number of men gathering stones to build themselves a house. But they could not lift what seemed to Ossian such little, light rocks. At last he could bear it no longer and leaned from his horse to give a push to a recalcitrant stone. As he touched it he turned to dust.

Another and more widely spread version of Ossian's end, however, makes him outlive all the Feinn. In this story he finally enters a hill with his mother and sleeps for 300 years. He is awakened by the sound of St. Patrick's bell, though his hill, so far as I know, is never described as being in Ireland. But then in legend St. Patrick came first to Scotland and only fled to Ireland when the witches of Scotland drove him out, throwing Dunbarton Rock after him. During his sleep Ossian was in 'cold Elphin' but he now becomes a resident in one of St. Patrick's monasteries and does not like it at all. He comments sadly on the dreariness of monastic life. 'Too much fast, and drowsy sound of bell,' he says. Ossian ran nine skewers into his stomach to restrain his appetite, but even then he was getting the food of fifteen men and was still hungry. He came out of his cell to help some builders and lifted a lintel-stone above a door which fifteen warriors could not handle. 'That was the best feat', said they. 'If the people inside gave me the food of sixteen men that were no feat', answered Ossian. Finally he obtained an interview with St. Patrick, with whom he held a disputation. According to the *Dialogue of the Ancients* (eleventh century) St. Patrick having said that Fionn must be in Hell, Ossian replied: Fionn, King of Feinn, the Generous One, was without blemish. All the qualities which you and your clerics say are according to the rule of the King of the Stars, Fionn's Fenians had them all; and if they are in pain, great would be the shame, for if God Himself would be in bonds, my Chief would fight on His behalf. Fionn never suffered anyone to be in pain or difficulty and can his doom be Hell, in the House of Cold?' (Fionn, it seems, was threatened with the cold hell of the Northern gods, a place of ice and wind and darkness ruled over by Hel herself, and not with our Eastern hell of fire and brimstone.)

Ossian then bitterly laments the passing of Fionn and his times. The *Lament of Ossian in his Old Age* has been preserved in the *Book of the Dean of Lismore* (sixteenth century) and translated by Dr Douglas Hyde. Here is an extract:

> Long was last night in cold Elphin,
> More long is tonight on its weary way.
> Though yesterday seemed to me long and ill,
> Yet longer still was this weary day.
>
> And long for me is each hour new-born,
> Stricken, forlorn and smit with grief
> For the hunting lands and the Fenian bands
> And the long-haired, generous Fenian Chief.
>
> I hear no music, I find no feast,
> I slay no beast from a bounding steed.
> I bestow no gold, I am poor and old,
> I am sick and cold, without wine or mead.

I court no more, I hunt no more,
These were before my strong delight,
I cannot slay, and I take no prey,
Weary the day and long the night.

No heroes come in their war array,
No game I play, there is naught to win,
I swim no stream with my men of might,
Long is the night in cold Elphin.

Ask, O Patrick, thy God of Grace
To tell me the place he will place me in,
And save my soul from the Ill One's might
For long is tonight in cold Elphin.

St. Patrick offers Ossian baptism and Heaven but he decides he does not want to be saved and go alone to Heaven but to rejoin Fionn and the Feinn at the Last Day. This is his prayer. St. Patrick at last assures him that he will after all meet Fionn and his Feinn in Heaven, their good deeds having saved them. Ossian then agrees to be baptised for them all and as the holy water touches him he dies.

On every New Year's Eve, at that moment between the years when there is no time and no man can be born or die, the Feinn meet again on the top of Mamratagan. But for them the moment lasts until the first dawn flash comes up over the hills to the east. This is their reward for never turning their backs on an enemy in battle, never harming a woman, never betraying a man. For this they are allowed to leave cold Elphin where some say, being pagans, they have to spend the time between their own deaths and the world's end. Others, however, think that St. Patrick kept his promise to Ossian and they are all in Heaven, but that even there they are homesick for the Highlands.

From the top of Mamratagan the road winds down a long steep hill into the green valley of Glenelg. And anyone who looks across the water to Skye and at the other views which open out to east and west as one descends the hill will realise why those who belong to the Highlands will always be homesick for them, wheresoever they may be.